How to Teach Thinking and Learning Skills

A Practical Programme for the Whole School

C. J. Simister

P·C·P

Paul Chapman
Publishing

Paul Chapman Publishing
A SAGE Publications Company
1 Oliver's Yard
55 City Road
London EC1Y 1SP

SAGE Publications Inc
2455 Teller Road
Thousand Oaks, California 91320

SAGE Publications India Pvt Ltd
B 1/I1 Mohan Cooperative Industrial Area
Mathura Road, Post Bag 7
New Delhi 110 044

SAGE Publications Asia-Pacific Pte Ltd
33 Pekin Street #02–01
Far East Square
Singapore 048763

Library of Congress Control Number: 2007924069

British Library Cataloguing in Publication Data

A catalogue record for this book is available from the British Library

ISBN 978-1-4129-3421-3
ISBN 978-1-4129-3422-0 (pbk)

Typeset by C&M Digitals (P) Ltd, Chennai, India
Printed in Great Britain by The Cromwell Press, Trowbridge, Wiltshire
Printed on paper from sustainable resources

Contents

Contents of the CD Rom

THINK! Skills Overview – full-colour version

Lesson resources for the THINK! programme

Year 1

My Magical Thinking Potion	Activity sheet
The Good Thinker Game	Teacher instructions
The Good Thinker Game	Activity cards (3 pages)
Star Questions	Poster
Star Questions about …	Activity sheet (curriculum follow-up)
Questioning for Understanding	Poster
Questioning for Understanding – picture sheet	Activity sheet
Questioning for Understanding – sample dialogues	Teacher instructions
Odd One Out	Activity cards (5 pages)
What am I?	Teacher instructions
What am I? cards	Activity cards (2 pages)
Patchwork Thinking	Activity sheet (curriculum follow-up)
Start with a Squiggle!	Teacher instructions
Use it or lose it!	Activity sheet (for more able/older pupils)
Target Board – perfect pet	Activity sheet
Target Board picture cards	Activity cards (7 pages)
Target Board	Activity sheet (curriculum follow-up)
All Ears!	Teacher instructions
All Ears!	Activity sheet

Year 2

First to Find …	Teacher instructions
First to Find …	Activity sheet
How can you recognise a good learner?	Activity sheet
Good Learner cards	Activity cards (2 pages)
Three 'Whys' Men	Teacher instructions
What do you wonder?	Activity sheet
What do you *really* want to know?	Activity sheet (for more able/older pupils)
Six Steps to Success	Activity sheet
Six Steps to Success challenge cards	Activity cards
Thinking with flow diagrams	Activity sheet
Flow diagram pictures	Activity cards
Tied Up in Knots!	Teacher instructions

All activities on this CD Rom can be printed out and are copyright © C. J. Simister 2007, Paul Chapman Publishing.

Key for icons

Grouping for lesson plans

Whole class discussion   D

Whole class activity   C

Group activity (single digit number shows   G4
suggested size, e.g. 4 here)

Individual   I

Icons on lesson plans

On accompanying CD Rom

Helpful hints

Display suggestions

Link to source

Brain characters

Each of the seven brain characters represents a different part of the thinking programme. They are:

Metacognition

Questioning

Information skills

Critical thinking

Creative thinking

Decision making

Memory skills

Preface

I haven't met many teachers who don't wholeheartedly want their students to develop their potential as individuals capable of self-directed, rigorous and original thought. Rarely is our aim simply to churn out exam-passing automatons. I have, however, frequently been asked how to go about this – particularly when we are so often operating within a system that primarily rewards high grades, regardless of the level of thought that is needed to achieve them.

While there is no easy answer to this question, there are several shifts that, if encouraged, can clearly make an enormous difference. First, the shift from teaching as a didactic process to learning as a communal experience, where the teacher is engaged in the wonder of thinking together with his or her pupils. Secondly, the shift in primary focus away from subject content towards those life-long skills and dispositions that will equip and encourage the learner to continue learning – well beyond the dates of any school examinations. And thirdly, the shift in belief that intelligence is pretty much fixed towards the recognition that we shape our brains with every new experience we encounter, every challenge we overcome and every risk we take.

Let's hope that one day we will re-design our entire education experience based upon these shifts. In the meantime, this book is for those teachers who want to make a start within the existing system. It offers a wealth of practical ideas for how to develop children's thinking and learning skills, both through one-off activities and games and by approaching curriculum subjects in a different and more interactive way. The lessons have been tried and tested: they are engaging and effective, as well as simple to implement. The programme that is described can just as easily be followed by a whole school intending to engage in a genuine culture change, as by an individual wanting to change the way that he or she teaches, learns, thinks.

This book contains 42 lesson plans and a sample of their supporting resources. More than 100 activity instruction sheets, pupil worksheets, cards, posters and certificates can be found on the accompanying CD Rom, as indicated by the 🌑 icon.

C. J. Simister

Acknowledgements

The author and publishers would like to thank the following (listed alphabetically):

Tony Buzan – for granting permission to include Mind Maps (Year 3, Lesson 3)
Mind Map® is a registered trademark of the Buzan Organisation Limited 1990. For more information contact: BUZAN CENTRES WORLDWIDE PLC, www.Buzancentresworldwide.com.

Brent Clark for the illustrations, which appear on the activity sheets on the CD Rom.

Guy Claxton – for his inspiring talks at both the 10th and 12th International Conferences on Thinking in Harrogate and Melbourne and for his encouragement with this book. Many thanks also to his publishers, TLO Limited, for granting permission to include concepts and ideas from Guy Claxton's Building Learning Power (BLP) programme. The BLP resources are thoroughly recommended to anyone who is interested in developing a genuine, effective and lasting emphasis on learning to learn within their school. Visit www.buildinglearningpower.co.uk for further information.

Anne de A'Echevarria – for her permission to include the Target Board tool (Year 1, Lesson 6).

Robert Fisher – for visiting our school and launching our thinking and learning skills programme in 2004 and for his suggestion that I write this book. His publishers, Nelson Thornes and Nash Pollock Publishing, are also thanked for their permission to include several ideas from his books in this programme (Mystery Voices – Year 1, Lesson 7; Spot the Difference! – Year 2, Lesson 7; Disconnect! – Year 5, Lesson 4; What could it be? – Year 5, Lesson 6). For further details of Robert Fisher's many extremely useful resources, visit http://www.teachingthinking.net/.

Mike Fleetham – for permission to use Patchwork Thinking (Year 1, Lesson 4). Visit www.thinkingclassroom.co.uk for more free Thinking Skills resources.

David Fulton Publishers – for permission to include Layers of Inference (Year 6, Lesson 4).

Michael Gruneberg – for permission to refer to his Link Word technique for learning languages (Year 3, Lesson 7).

Institute of Education, London – for the support of my tutors, Caroline Lodge and Chris Watkins, whose first job was to organise *my* thinking skills and who provided such thoughtful advice and encouragement throughout my MA.

János Márffy – for the hours spent creating the 'brain character' icons that are used throughout this book. János can be contacted at: janos.marffy@mosaik.info.hu.

The *Daily Telegraph* – for granting permission to quote their article in the illustration on page 6.

Thinking Maps Inc. – for allowing the inclusion of the Multi-Flow Map (Year 5, Lesson 4). The Multi-Flow Map is one of eight Thinking Maps®, a common visual language owned by Thinking Maps, Inc. Thinking Maps® is a registered trademark of Thinking Maps, Inc.

And finally, the author would like to acknowledge the teachers at Northwood College for their work in turning these ideas and many others into reality in their everyday lessons. For further information about the school and its innovative thinking and learning skills programme, visit: www.northwoodcollege.co.uk.

Every effort has been made to contact copyright holders of materials reproduced in this book. The author and publishers apologise for any omissions and will be pleased to rectify them at the earliest opportunity.

About the author

C. J. Simister is the director of an extensive programme of thinking and learning skills at Northwood College, Middlesex. After reading Economics at Cambridge University, she trained as a teacher and gained wide-ranging experience of classroom practice, working in both state and independent sectors and with pupils from primary age to sixth form. Following a Masters degree in School Effectiveness and Improvement at the Institute of Education in London, she published papers in the field of thinking skills and gifted education and took up her current position in 2004. Northwood College's Advanced Cognitive Development Programme appeared in the magazine *Teaching Thinking and Creativity*. She presented it at the International Conference on Thinking in Melbourne in July 2005 and chaired a thinking skills conference in Singapore in March 2006. C. J. Simister also runs Creative and Critical Thinking Holiday Workshops, sometimes in conjunction with the National Association of Gifted Children (NAGC).

Part One

Thinking about Learning and Learning about Thinking

Chapter 1

What does this book offer?

'Most people would rather die than think. In fact, they do,' claimed Bertrand Russell. Possibly a slight exaggeration! Nevertheless, one that may bring a smile to the faces of the many teachers who feel they are fighting a constant battle against their students' longing to be told exactly what to write, what to learn, what to think.

Try it for yourself. Do any of the following traits sound familiar?

Are there pupils in your class who …

- Prefer you to tell them exactly what to write and feel uncomfortable unless there is one 'right answer'?
- Either lack the confidence to put forward their own ideas or have plenty of confidence, but don't think before they speak?
- Swing between waiting for you to tell them what to do next and making rash decisions without thinking through the options?
- Dislike problem solving because they have to work out for themselves the best method to use?
- Assume learning should be fast and easy – and judge themselves as failures when it isn't and they sometimes get things wrong?

If so, you are not alone. Our pupils have many wonderful traits, but independent thinking is sadly rare. The question is – why is this snapshot so familiar? Well, in part, it probably describes a natural and fairly prevalent human characteristic – the unwillingness to do more than we need in any given situation. Or put another way – laziness!

However, it is likely that matters are being made worse by three more recent trends:

- The trend towards an increasingly prescriptive curriculum.
- The trend towards judging pupils by the number of examination hurdles over which they can jump.
- The trend towards judging schools by overly simplistic league tables.

> The brain is a wonderful organ; it starts the moment you get up in the morning and does not stop until you get to the office.
>
> Robert Frost
> (American poet,
> 1874–1963)

Each of these is acting in concert to mean that it may not, after all, be the students' fault.

There is a saying that children enter school as question marks and leave as full stops. Something happens during this phase of life – a diminishing curiosity, a desire to conform rather than stand out, an increasing unwillingness to take risks. While we can certainly attribute it in part to adolescent hormones, in part to society, in part simply to 'growing up', we should not ignore the fact that one of the contributing factors is very likely to be **what takes place in schools**. As McPeck put it, 'Children are not fools: if regurgitation and getting the right answer are what bring high marks, then that is what they will do' (1990: 51).

There has been, over the past few years in particular, a growing interest in the field of thinking and learning skills. While some may argue that children should be developing such skills automatically through the enquiry and analysis demanded by the various school subjects, others suggest this is an idealistic assumption which may be limiting the scope of children's educational experience. Should we be re-assessing our methods and approaches to make sure we are doing all we can to support the development of our students' cognitive processes and abilities?

While the debate has raged, a growing wealth of approaches has developed, each of which offers something new and valuable to the thinking and learning skills story. And, more recently, the UK's 'Decade of the Brain' provoked a flurry of interest in the potential gains that may eventually result from the application of the latest brain imaging techniques and understanding to educational practice.

Many schools are keen to investigate what all of this might mean in practice. Educators have an instinctive idea that teaching pupils to be independent, creative and critical thinkers who can take control of their own learning is surely 'a good thing'. Furthermore, the DfES endorses the idea, offering a list of thinking skills, together with guidance regarding methods that can be used. Indeed, there is now a vast and often bewildering tangle of ideas and material being published within the field of thinking and learning skills – some good, some less so. The problem is that very few teachers have the time to plough through the many books and Internet sites that offer suggestions and, with so much information available, developing a thinking and learning skills focus can seem a rather daunting prospect.

So, to return to the original question ... What does *this* book offer?

1.   This book offers a clear and practical way forward for schools

The programme described here is innovative but easy to use, either by individual class teachers who have an interest in the subject or by schools who want to develop a shared approach that gives greater attention to thinking and learning skills.

2.   The programme is rooted in sound educational theory

The programme is the product of several years of sifting through the vast array of material that exists, as well as adapting, improving and creating new techniques. As a result, it is packed full of great ideas and resources. Basically, it has done the hard work for you.

3.   It is extremely flexible

You might choose any of the following options:

- Dip in and pick out the activities that you would like to try. Although presented as a programme for different year groups, almost all the techniques are suitable for a range of ages, with a little adaptation. The table 'Thinking and learning skills strategies and games', in Part Two on pages 32–3, gives a useful overview of the wide range of approaches that are described.
- Focus on one class only and use that year group's lesson plans.
- Follow the programme across several or all year groups.
- Extend the programme's impact significantly by referring back to the lesson plans of previous year groups and continuing to use and develop these strategies in later classes, together with the methods suggested for that year.

4. The techniques work

The lesson plans are based on ideas that have been developed and trialled with pupils at Northwood College, Middlesex. Its highly innovative thinking skills programme was described in the magazine *Teaching Thinking and Creativity* and it attracted much interest from schools around the world when presented at the International Conference on Thinking, in Melbourne July 2005 and in Singapore in March 2006.

5. Your pupils will enjoy it!

This is a programme for all pupils. The techniques have been found to appeal enormously to pupils across a range of abilities, learning approaches and personalities. As the content is predominantly skills-based, the activities are 'equalising' by nature, allowing all to respond at their own levels. Differentiation occurs by outcome, often with surprising results. Pupils appreciate the message that *everyone* can learn to be a better thinker and a more effective learner.

To paraphrase Edward de Bono, you may be lucky enough to have been born with a Ferrari of a brain, but you can still crash it into a tree. It's what we learn to *do* with our natural abilities that makes by far the most difference.

This book certainly does not claim to provide an exhaustive list of every method that exists. Critical Thinking, for an example, is a subject in its own right and the ideas included here simply introduce and develop the type of logical reasoning that forms a background for these skills. However, it does suggest a starting point for schools who recognise the importance of helping their pupils to become independent thinkers and learners, but who are not quite sure how best to proceed. Put simply, it offers schools one clear route through the jungle. After that, it will be up to each school to decide whether they would also like to explore other directions.

Chapter 2

Why should we *teach* thinking and learning skills?

You might ask why we should be *teaching* thinking and learning skills? Don't children think and learn already? The response is that of course children develop their thinking and learning skills while at school, regardless of whether these are given specific focus. It would be extremely worrying if this were not the case. The question is simply: is this enough or could we do more?

Well, let's begin by looking at the alternative. Sticking with things as they are. Students are passing through school, learning their subjects, carrying out their course work and sitting their exams. A greater proportion than ever before are achieving A grades and a higher number are going into further education. Surely this is a sign of success?

We all certainly hope so. However, we must ask ourselves whether grades and university entrance statistics paint an entirely reliable picture of what's happening. For a start, if this were the case, surely we would expect universities and employers to be delighted with so many highly achieving students? And yet frequently the headlines suggest otherwise ...

Daily Telegraph, 9 February 2006
Management-Issues, 20 July 2006

Might there be a danger that we are sacrificing the longer-term potential of our students for short-term gains in terms of school success? By focusing permanently on covering the syllabus, on force-feeding the information required, on cramming for examinations, are we moulding the thinkers and learners of the future or churning out mediocre automatons?

Professor Robert Fisher suggests:

There is evidence that traditional teaching methods are efficient in teaching what the Greeks called *tekne*, the 'technical' side of knowing how to do and make things, the basic skills and techniques which need to be introduced and practised by beginners in any area of learning. But traditional methods are less successful in developing what the Greeks called *phronesis*, that is practical wisdom or intelligence, the higher order thinking which enhances skill to the level of expertise. (2003: 18)

> We should not be preparing our students for a life of tests but for the test of life.

Art Costa, Harrogate Conference, 2002

This is not a new problem. In de Botton's book *The Consolations of Philosophy*, he quotes the sixteenth-century French philosopher Montaigne, who wrote:

> I gladly come back to the theme of the absurdity of our education: its end has not been to make us good and wise, but learned ... We ought to find out not who understands *most* but who understands *best* ... We work merely to fill the memory. (quoted in de Botton, 2000: 153)

And still earlier, the ancient Greek philosopher Heraclitus wrote, 'Knowing many things doesn't teach insight' (quoted in von Oech, 1998: 209).

Perhaps it all hinges on what we mean by thinking. Our students do think. But they don't think as well as they could.

What are the arguments for teaching thinking and learning?

1. To attempt to keep alight the curiosity and creativity seen in young children.

Curiosity is one of the most permanent and certain characteristics of a vigorous mind

Samuel Johnson
Writer and lexicographer, 1708–1784

What is proved was once only imagined

William Blake
Poet and artist, 1752–1827

Discovery consists of looking at the same thing as everyone else and thinking something different

Albert Szent Gyorgyi
Physiologist and Nobel Laureate, 1893–1986

2. To encourage children to stand out from the crowd, to take risks and put forward their own ideas, to make suggestions, to offer opinions and not be put off by a fear of 'getting it wrong' or 'looking stupid'.

If you think there is only one right answer, then you'll stop looking as soon as you find one

Roger von Oech
A Whack on the Side of the Head, 1998

3. To enhance the quality, complexity and inventiveness of children's thinking instead of teaching them to regurgitate other people's words and solutions.

Nothing is more dangerous than an idea when it is the only one you have

Emile Chartier
Philosopher, *Propos sur la religion*, 1938

Doubt is not a pleasant condition. But certainty is absurd

Voltaire
Enlightenment writer, 1694–1778

4. To promote open-mindedness and tolerance.

It's not that I'm so smart, it's just that I stay with problems longer

Albert Einstein
Theoretical physicist and Nobel Laureate, 1879–1955

5. To build a more dynamic view of intelligent behaviour as something that can be developed by everyone rather than a quality reserved for a privileged few.

6. To boost morale and motivation: the approaches are lively and entertaining and encourage children to take a more active role in their own education.

This means we can pack our thinking bags and be ready to explore life!

Jenna, age 10

As teachers, we have ... produced tabloid fodder. Year after year our school leavers become full members of society and yet they seem to bring no higher an expectation of autonomy to the minds of the mass-selling newspaper editors who seek sales, to the politicians who seek their vote and the advertisers who seek their cash

Victor Quinn
Critical Thinking in Young Minds, 1997

7. To teach children to reason: to avoid gullibility and to reach informed and balanced decisions and opinions.

The mark of an educated mind is to be able to entertain an idea without accepting it

Aristotle
Greek philosopher, 384–322 S.C

8. To help children learn to respond to a rapidly changing world, where the ability to make sense of new information, to think creatively and to solve problems are increasingly valuable.

Even if you are on the right track, you will get run over if you just sit there

Will Rogers
Humorist and showman,
1879–1935

We need to educate pupils for jobs that don't yet exist

Robert Fisher
10th International Conference on
Thinking, 2002

Learning seeks to reduce uncertainty, by transmuting the strange into the familiar, but it also needs to tolerate uncertainty as the seedbed in which ideas germinate and responses form

Guy Claxton
Hare Brain, Tortoise Mind, 1997

9. To help create lifelong learners by preparing children to face the uncertainty and open-endedness that comes with a true spirit of enquiry.

10. To help children achieve their intellectual potential.

Thinking is the hardest work there is, which is probably the reason why so few engage in it

Henry Ford
Founder of the Ford Motor Co.,
1863–1947

Chapter 3

What are thinking and learning skills?

We probably all have a similar idea of what we would like to see. Students who engage in careful, reflective, skilful, quality thinking; students who are interested in the world and are motivated to pursue this curiosity and learn independently; students who have the courage to bring their own perspectives into the debate, to hone their ideas, to push forward the boundaries of understanding. But can these broad descriptions be broken down into 'teachable skills'?

The phrases 'thinking skills' and 'learning to learn' are used to mean a variety of things. For instance, the DfES classifies thinking skills as:

- Enquiry
- Information processing
- Creative thinking
- Reasoning
- Evaluation

And Professor Guy Claxton, author of *Building Learning Power*, defines its 'four Rs' as:

- Resilience – being ready, willing and able to lock on to learning
- Resourcefulness – being ready, willing and able to learn in different ways
- Reflectiveness – being ready, willing and able to become more strategic about learning
- Reciprocity – being ready, willing and able to learn alone or with other people

How are thinking and learning skills defined in *this* book?

Broadly speaking, the phrase 'thinking and learning skills' is used in this book to refer to the wide range of acquirable habits and skills that can help us to become more effective in the way we:

(a) gather and absorb information (learning skills); *and*
(b) transform this knowledge and generate new ideas (thinking skills).

There is clearly much overlap between the two areas, as we cannot learn without thinking, nor think without learning. However, the distinction can be a useful one as it is possible to be a highly skilled 'learner' who has underdeveloped analytical and creative thinking skills; similarly one can be an innovative thinker without the learning techniques to make the most of that potential.

Any definition of thinking and learning is bound to over-simplify. However, by dividing what is a huge field into eight key areas, this book aims to provide a framework that strikes a balance between being both comprehensive and manageable. A description of seven of these stages can be found on page 12, with the final and arguably most important stage – metacognition – being discussed on page 13. Note that problem solving is not defined as a separate skill, as it represents the whole cycle, requiring a combination of questioning, gathering information, thinking critically and creatively, then making and communicating a decision.

This process, starting with questioning and resulting in communicating a decision or solution, represents a cycle of thinking and learning. Each decision that's made, each problem that's solved, is likely to throw up more questions and further issues to explore and investigate. Learning is a continual process and one that we hope our pupils will enjoy enough to choose to pursue well beyond the traditional cut-off of school examinations.

Two further overview sheets are provided at the beginning of Part Two: one that offers a detailed breakdown of the thinking and learning skills that are covered (THINK! skills overview, page 31) and one that lists all the methods used to address them (Thinking and learning skills strategies and games, pages 32–3). Versions of both are also available on the accompanying CD Rom.

Key Areas Covered in the Programme

QUESTIONING

This lies at the heart of thinking and learning, yet too often in schools it's the teacher who asks the questions and the pupil who answers them.

By turning this around, by encouraging children to think about the questions *they* would like to explore, we help them see learning as an active and exciting process and one that they can play a part in directing.

After all, this is where research starts – with someone who raises a new question; this is where new inventions are created – with someone who asks how things could be improved; and this is where progress is initiated – with someone who questions the status quo.

COMMUNICATION

We need to teach pupils to listen to each other, to work together collaboratively to reach group decisions, to negotiate, to compromise and to build better ideas by drawing from what they hear rather than sticking stubbornly to one point of view.

They must learn to present their own opinions articulately and to be able to justify these intelligently, while also being flexible enough to change their mind if new information alters the picture.

MEMORY SKILLS

Research has shown that we can dramatically improve our memories and it's surprising that the simple techniques that have been devised are not taught in schools.

Instead, we find too often that children rely on reading and re-reading their notes, when a more active approach can prove more fun, as well as be considerably more effective.

INFORMATION SKILLS

The next two driving forces are information and ideas – and they feed off each other.

Children need to learn how to gather information from the vast quantity that is now readily available. They must find out how to sift through it, how to sort, summarise, sequence and prioritise the key points. They should be taught a range of methods of presenting information clearly and logically, so that their chance of reaching a genuine understanding is maximised.

DECISION MAKING

And so, questioning has led to gathering and processing information. Information has been critically assessed and new, innovative ideas have been added. A decision now needs to be made.

Children should be taught how to take this step with confidence in their reasoning. Options need to be listed, pros and cons weighed up, possible outcomes and consequences evaluated, different opinions and points of view taken into consideration. Decisions may not always be right, but if they are properly considered, at least the chances of success are improved.

CRITICAL THINKING

Linked to this – and overlapping to a significant extent – are the skills of critical or logical thinking.

Young people need to learn to be discerning with what they find: to clarify, to challenge, to evaluate competing positions, to assess logic and validity, to sort the sense from the nonsense. In teaching these skills, we help our students replace vulnerability with reason.

CREATIVE THINKING

Broadly speaking, ideas come in two forms: critical and creative – with the latter category sadly underplayed in schools. Too often, we are content with being the critical assessors of the world in which we live, rather than the inventors, the risk-takers, the bridge-builders.

We need the children of today to be the problem solvers of tomorrow – and that won't happen simply by picking to pieces other people's ideas.

A few words about 'metacognition': the missing eighth ingredient

Separating metacognition from the other strands of the programme is rather problematic. In reality, metacognition – or thinking about one's thinking – should permeate each and every stage of the process. It is arguably the mystery ingredient that has the power to determine how successful any thinking and learning skills approach will be. We can teach any number of tools and methods, but without metacognition these will simply join the list of 'things to repeat while at school'.

It is vital that students are encouraged to recognise and reflect upon the different thinking and learning skills that they're using, to learn which represent areas of strength for them and which need greater focus, to identify situations where these skills and methods are going to be valuable and situations where they won't. Basically, we want them to become fluent in the language of thinking and learning. Which means not just using the words, but understanding the context, the relevance and the implications for everyday life.

This type of reflection is the seed bed from which character traits form, change and grow. The habits and dispositions of an active thinker and learner need to be nurtured: they are specific and powerful and less likely to develop without attention. Character traits such as resilience, courage, curiosity, perseverance, humour, confidence and humility – these are far more important than any set of thinking and learning tools. The ideal, however, is to find a way of bringing the two together. Then you have something exciting.

By shifting the focus from knowledge to understanding, from absorbing to constructing, from observing to participating, we hope to equip pupils with a set of skills that not only will help them with their education, but will prepare them for their future.

Why is this the 'right' method to choose? Can't thinking and learning mean different things to different people?

There's no simple answer to the question 'What are thinking and learning skills?'. This book offers one means of breaking down the vast amount of theory into more manageable categories that follow a logical pattern and progression. However, while there may well be other ways of listing and grouping the ideas and skills, it's likely that the underlying principles will remain very much the same.

As an illustration of this, it is recommended that those schools that genuinely wish to transform their approach and to embark on a major thinking and learning skills initiative begin by engaging *everyone* in an exploration of the language that will be involved. Language can be a powerful binding force, but equally well, it has the capacity to exclude. Words that seem perfectly normal to one set of people may be unrecognisable to another – with the result that some may feel alienated and resentful.

One way of introducing such an exploration is to use American psychologist B.F. Skinner's comment (1964) that education is what survives when you've forgotten all that you learned as a stimulus for staff discussions, perhaps as an INSET activity. (You may like to use the photocopiable resource on page 14.) By asking for everyone's ideas about what *should* be left over, a fascinating discussion can be prompted. At a time when there are many divisions and debates within education, it can be heartening to discover that teachers are often surprisingly united in their belief about what education should ultimately be about.

A school that takes the time to engage in this sort of activity will find that it develops its own interpretation of what thinking and learning skills actually involve. This is an important step along the path towards deeper level cultural change. This process of 'demystification' allows everyone to see that, even though different words may sometimes be used, we are all likely to be working towards the same goal.

How much can you *really* remember of what you learned at school?

Of all the things you learned while at school, what has been most helpful?

Education is what survives when you've forgotten all that you learned.

After B.F. Skinner, *New Scientist*, 21 May 1964

What do you think *should* 'survive'?

What do you wish *you* had been taught at school?

Chapter 4

How do you teach thinking and learning?

There is much debate about how thinking and learning skills should be taught. Should they be taught separately or integrated into the curriculum? The response of this author is: Why argue? Let's do both.

For three reasons:

1   How can we be *sure* that traditional subjects provide the best context for developing the thinking and learning skills that we hope will become second nature? After all, these subjects don't represent everything there is to think about. Indeed, it could be argued that our insistence on restricting ourselves to such tightly compartmentalised 'subject boxes' reflects an educational system still very much ensnarled by its historical roots rather than one that recognises the interactive and fluid nature of the world in which we now live. Thinking and learning skills are not context specific: there are real, practical tools and dispositions that have value far beyond the range of disciplines provided in schools.

2   When we teach reading, we do so by introducing children to the basic skills within imaginative child-friendly contexts – stories, poems, cartoons … It's not until they become more confident that we begin to move them on to more traditionally 'academic' subjects. Why not begin by introducing children to new ways of thinking and learning against backgrounds that are more innately child-friendly: favourite television shows, stories, hobbies and interests?

3   Having said that, it would clearly be absurd *not to* apply them to the curriculum as well, given that it remains at the heart of our education system and contains much that is of very great value.

For these reasons, the programme outlined in this book is based on the belief that, to have a real chance of improving the quality of your pupils' thinking and learning, these skills should:

- be taught initially as a separate subject rooted in unthreatening topics of immediate interest to pupils
- thereafter, gradually be embedded in the curriculum and in the everyday contexts of life

The THINK! programme 'starter kit'

As explained earlier, it's perfectly possible for a teacher simply to open up this book and select an idea or technique from virtually any of the lesson plans. However, for schools wishing to develop a more continuous and comprehensive programme, it offers a 'starter kit' for each year group (from Year 1 to Year 6), which includes:

- One lesson plan that focuses on developing pupils' metacognition, with suggestions for follow-up activities:

    (a)   to help pupils identify and develop the dispositions that frequently underpin successful thinking and learning
    (b)   to increase their awareness of themselves as thinkers and learners
    (c)   to increase familiarity with the language needed to evaluate their own thinking and learning

- Six further lessons plans, one for each of the main thinking and learning areas of the programme overview:

    o   Questioning
    o   Information skills
    o   Critical thinking
    o   Creative thinking
    o   Decision making
    o   Memory skills

Each of the six lesson plans develops a specific thinking or learning skill by introducing two practical strategies: one as a warm-up game and the other as a more extended activity. Suggestions are then included for follow-up lessons, which integrate these strategies into a variety of curriculum subjects. To gain the maximum from this programme, teachers are strongly encouraged to be as flexible and creative as possible in thinking of additional contexts for follow-up lessons that are relevant to their topics of study.

This means that, by following this programme, each year group has the opportunity to introduce a significant range of new thinking and learning tools which can then be used as frequently as teachers wish within their own topics and curriculum subjects.

Furthermore, it is recommended that teachers look back at the tools and ideas suggested for earlier years. These very frequently suit older pupils just as well, if not more, and their value will be greatly enhanced by their integration throughout the school, rather than as a one-off method in one year group alone. Some of the lesson plans contain specific notes for use by other year groups and the list of thinking and learning skills strategies and games in Part Two on pages 32–3 provides a useful resource for teachers wishing to do this.

Chapter 5

How do I use the THINK! programme in practice?

The structure of a typical lesson

As explained in the previous chapter, each year group is provided with seven lesson plans that can be used at any time during the school year. Each lesson follows the same format, using the acronym 'THINK!' as a structure:

T	Tune in!	5/10 minute warm up game or activity
H	Heads together	20 minute philosophical discussion
I	Investigate	25/30 minute focus on a particular thinking or learning skill
N	Now reflect!	5 minute opportunity for reflection
K	Keep thinking	Task for pupils to do at home or in spare time

The lesson plans, each of which covers two pages, can be found in Part Two. Virtually all the necessary resources are provided on the CD Rom – teacher instructions, pupil sheets and activity cards. These are listed at the end of each year group's section, together with a selection of 'At a Glance' reduced-size pictures of activity sheets for reference.

The timings given in the table above are approximate and lessons would usually take between 60 and 90 minutes to work through all the stages. However, the programme is extremely flexible and teachers may prefer to carry out the 'Heads together' or the 'Investigate' section on different days if the time available is shorter. They may find that activities take longer than expected (this can easily happen, as it often seems a shame to cut short a lively discussion or a successful activity), in which case lessons can be spread across several sessions, or teachers can pick out those parts that they wish to focus on and leave out other elements.

Although the lessons are designed with whole-class teaching in mind, sometimes teachers may prefer to adapt the activities and work with one group at a time. This approach would suit Year 1 particularly well and may also be preferable with Year 2. A classroom assistant may be able to take the activity or free up the teacher to give his or her full attention to one group at a time, monitoring what they are doing and how they are thinking, as well as guiding the activity as appropriate. What is important is that whoever does the activity is well grounded in the teaching approach that is most likely to maximise the benefits of the activities (see Question Eight in Chapter 6, page 24)

Curriculum application

For the follow-up lessons, it is recommended that teachers:

- Repeat or adapt the same 'Tune in!' activity in most instances
- Incorporate a suitable discussion activity (for a detailed explanation of the 'Heads together' element of the lessons, see the following section)
- Use the suggestions provided to consider how the strategy can best fit within their own class's curriculum and topics

In this way, your pupils will be introduced to two new thinking and learning activities, which will then be reinforced within a more academic context. It is this paired planning structure which has been found to make the programme particularly effective.

How does the 'Heads together' section work?

Within the activities described in the seven lessons for each year group, there are plenty of opportunities for pupils to discuss and present the ideas that they develop. However, the 'Heads together' component of the programme offers a further, more specific context for your pupils to develop their communication and reasoning skills.

Through the use of a highly regarded discussion method – Philosophy for Children – your pupils gain valuable experience of listening and responding to each other, of forming and expressing their own opinions and of reaching decisions.

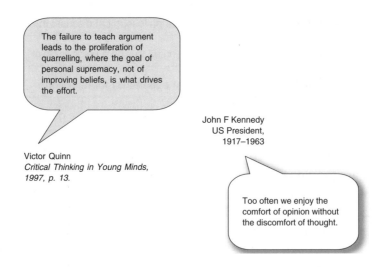

The failure to teach argument leads to the proliferation of quarrelling, where the goal of personal supremacy, not of improving beliefs, is what drives the effort.

Victor Quinn
Critical Thinking in Young Minds,
1997, p. 13.

John F Kennedy
US President,
1917–1963

Too often we enjoy the comfort of opinion without the discomfort of thought.

Philosophy for Children (P4C)

Philosophy for Children was originally developed by Professor Matthew Lipman and his associates at the Institute for the Advancement of Philosophy for Children in New Jersey, USA during the late 1960s and early 1970s. It is supported in the UK by the education charity SAPERE (Society for the Advancement of Philosophical Enquiry and Reflection in Education), which began in the early 1990s following the televising of a programme about the work of Professor Lipman, entitled 'Socrates for 6 year olds'. This programme showed significant gains made by the children who took part in the P4C approach.

Philosophy for Children is now practised in more than 30 countries worldwide. It is an approach to developing discussion skills that has been thoroughly trialled in many schools and across all age groups.

The following procedure is recommended:

1   *'Heads together' Introductory Session*
     It is suggested that you spend the 'Heads together' section of Lesson 1 developing a series of class rules for the discussions.
2   *Generating the Question Session*
     First, introduce your class to a stimulus passage, short story, poem, news article, object or picture and allow them to generate and vote on a question to debate in the following session. The idea is that the children are involved and interested in the subject right from the start.
3   *Discussion Session*
     This can take place in the curriculum follow-up session or at a separate time. Focus on the question that was chosen, hold the discussion and reach individual and group decisions where possible. The teacher should play a 'back-seat' role as much as possible: selecting pupils to talk, ensuring that everyone keeps to the agreed rules and guiding the conversation if it becomes 'stuck in a rut' or diverts too much from the topic at hand. You may also wish to introduce the suggested discussion skill (a taxonomy of listening and speaking skills is provided in the 'Heads together: development of skills' table on page 34 in Part Two).

More detailed summary sheets for these three sessions, together with sample class rules and a list of suggested discussion topics and resources, can be found in Part Three on pages 146–51. The box below provides an example of how a 'Heads together' section appears in a lesson plan, this one taken from Year 3, Lesson 2.

Heads together

This lesson:	Philosophy for Children, 'Generating the Question Session'	Page 150
Curriculum lesson:	Philosophy for Children, 'Discussion Session'	Page 151
Discussion skill:	Expressing agreement and disagreement. Encourage your class to respond with 'I agree with … because …' and 'I disagree with … because …'	

An excellent book that gives a much more detailed, but still highly accessible overview of the Philosophy for Children approach is *Teaching Thinking: Philosophical Enquiry in the Classroom* by Robert Fisher (2003).

Should you wish to become a qualified Philosophy for Children practitioner, SAPERE provides P4C training courses for teachers, as well as several very valuable resources that give a much greater insight into the P4C process. To find out more, contact www.sapere.org.uk.

SAPERE also recommends the following books: *Thinking Together*, by Phil Cam (1995), *Children as Philosophers*, by Joanna Haynes (2002), *Teaching for Better Thinking*, by Laurence Splitter and Ann Sharp (1995). Full details are given in the references at the back of the book.

Chapter 6

Tips for success: questions and answers

The following questions and answers may help you to consider how this programme could be used most effectively within your school. A reflection sheet is also provided on p. 26.

Question One

Is it possible to use the lesson plans on their own without following them up within the curriculum?

While the lesson plans have been designed to stand alone if necessary, the tools should be integrated into the curriculum as much as possible in order to have a real impact on children's thinking and learning. This gives your pupils greater familiarity with the new ideas and illustrates their relevance within a range of contexts. A few suggestions are included in each lesson plan, but you may come up with applications that are much more directly suited to your class.

Question Two

What if it's just me who's interested? Can I use this book with one class or does it need to be applied across several year groups?

The programme can be adopted by a whole school, so that there is a clear development of skills across the year groups, but it is equally useful for a teacher operating on his or her own within a school.

Question Three

Do I need to use the lesson plans exactly as they are set out – for the recommended year group and in the recommended order?

Absolutely not. While the programme has been carefully designed to ensure a progression and balance of thinking and learning skills across the year groups, teachers will find that they can use not only the lesson plans for their particular year group, but also very many of the other lessons, with those in the years below their own being particularly easy to adapt to suit different ages. The table 'Thinking and learning skills strategies and games' on pages 32–3 in Part Two suggests which year groups could be introduced to each of the different methods.

Remember that, even in schools where the programme is being introduced across all year groups, it's a good idea to refer back to previous lessons to adapt ideas and strategies. This will mean that the pupils are building an ever-expanding toolkit of skills that are practised and developed so that they become second nature. The aim is that, ultimately, your pupils will know how to select for themselves the appropriate strategies to use in different contexts.

Question Four

Could the lessons be used with pupils over the age of 11?

Yes. Many of the tools and strategies can easily and successfully be adapted for use with pupils right up to Sixth Form age. What makes them so effective is that they introduce a different type of challenge into lessons, as well as greater opportunity for communication, decision making and independent learning.

Question Five

How much can I adapt the 'Heads together' section?

The two-step process required for the Philosophy for Children approach – choosing a question to focus on for the given stimulus and then discussing that question – can be used at any other time if you would rather take it out of the lesson plans provided. Given the time pressures of modern schools, you may prefer to combine the two stages and hold one full discussion lesson in PSHE or within a relevant subject lesson whenever an opportunity presents. The technique can very usefully be incorporated into your general teaching practice and certainly needs not be restricted to this particular slot of the lesson plans.

Question Six

If I decide to have a weekly lesson, does it matter when this is scheduled?

The ideal is to hold your lesson at a time when it is possible to over-run a little if an activity is taking longer than expected. Apart from this, the lessons work well for different reasons at different times of the day: as a kick-start at the beginning of a morning or afternoon; to raise energy levels in the middle of a longer session with your class; or as a positive way to end the day or week.

Question Seven

You mention the importance of 'metacognition' and developing good thinking and learning habits. What exactly are these?

There has been a great deal of research carried out to identify a set of behaviours that characterise people who are successful in school, work and everyday life. The list provided on page 23, '20 Dispositions of an Active Thinker and Learner', summarises the sort of dispositions that have been found to be important. It has been carefully derived from several sources, most notably the work of Art Costa and Bena Kallick, founders of the 'Habits of Mind' approach. The following websites contain much useful material:

http://www.habits-of-mind.net/   The official website
http://www.habitsofmind.org/   A useful Australian website providing support for schools

Other useful sources are: *Building Learning Power: Helping Young People to Become Good Learners* (Claxton, 2002) and *The Seven Habits of Highly Effective People* (Covey, 1989).

There are many ways of promoting the development of active thinking and learning dispositions in your school. You might consider:

- Displaying the set of disposition word cards (included on the CD Rom) in classrooms and communal areas. Although by no means exhaustive, these will help raise awareness in staff and children of the characteristics that your school values and can be used as a focus for questioning and discussion
- Using the Good Learner and Good Thinker Certificates (included on the CD Rom) to highlight and reward these behaviours
- Selecting one or two dispositions at a time as a focus across the school and making these the subject of assemblies, displays and activities
- Encouraging your children to keep 'Thinking and Learning Logs' to record their reflections on their journey towards becoming active thinkers and learners. Include structured tasks (such as asking them to make a 'Top 3' list of their best dispositions or to note an incident during the day when they found one of the dispositions particularly challenging), as well as opportunities for your pupils simply to record their own thoughts about their learning
- Asking your pupils for *their* ideas about how to help everyone develop the dispositions

More specific activities are also included in Lesson 1 for each of the year groups.

20 Dispositions of an Active Thinker and Learner ✇

By emphasising the behaviours listed here, the aim is to steer pupils away from the belief that being good at thinking and learning is limited to those who are conventionally 'clever'. Everyone – regardless of ability – can learn to improve their potential by developing positive thinking and learning dispositions.

- **Cooperation and collaboration**: a willingness to work with other people, to learn from different points of view and to form new ideas and plans by pooling talents

- **Concentration**: the ability to stay focused and avoid distractions

- **Courage and self-belief**: the confidence to put forward one's own suggestions and ideas and to stand by a reasoned opinion regardless of other people's reaction, knowing that many good ideas are initially ridiculed

- **Curiosity and enthusiasm**: an eagerness to ask questions, to explore beyond what is 'required' and to discover new things

- **Direction**: a sense of purpose, an awareness of one's own goals and the inclination to consider how these might best be achieved

- **Empathy**: a willingness to listen to others and to try to understand things from their perspective

- **Flexibility**: the ability to adapt, to generate alternatives and to change one's mind when new information or arguments are presented

- **Good judgement**: a desire to avoid gullibility and to think critically about ideas and information before deciding what to believe

- **Humility**: the willingness to be self-critical, to accept when one is on the wrong path, to seek help when it is needed and to learn from others

- **Humour**: an ability to laugh at oneself and keep a balanced perspective

- **Imagination**: an inclination to visualise, to dream, be creative with one's thoughts rather than to think within conventional boundaries

- **Independence and initiative**: an awareness of the strategies and options that are available and a willingness to reach one's own decisions and take actions based on these

- **An open mind**: a readiness to welcome unusual ideas even if they sound strange at first and to consider how existing ideas can be improved and adapted

- **Perseverance and tenacity**: a willingness to keep looking, keep thinking and keep learning rather than settling for the first plausible answer or idea that comes along

- **Precision**: the willingness to be careful, accurate and pay attention to detail

- **Reflectiveness**: an inclination to think about the methods and approaches that have been tried and to analyse both successes and failures

- **Resilience**: the confidence to 'stick with it' when thinking and learning 'hurt', to not give up at the first hurdle and to recognise the importance of intellectual struggling

- **Responsibility**: a recognition that each person is responsible for improving their own thinking and learning and for finding methods that suit them

- **Risk taking**: the courage to 'take a chance' and have a go at new things even when success may not be guaranteed

- **Self-discipline**: the self control required to make sure one's potential is achieved

Question Eight

Is any particular teaching approach recommended?

Although there is certainly no single 'right way' of teaching, your style of presentation will greatly affect the impact of the lessons. A few practical tips are:

1   Take the time to draw out your pupils' ideas, to value all suggestions, to work with what is offered and to use it in a positive way rather than dismissing any child's comment. It is important to remember that the aim is for your children to become confident thinkers as opposed to confident copiers – and this will only happen if you treat their thoughts with a great deal of care, nurturing them, directing them where necessary, and never squashing or ignoring them.
2   When praise is offered, it should be specific. Comment directly on your pupils' suggestions and dispositions, on their strengths and on those areas where further progress could be made.
3   Be prepared to model not just the methods, but also the dispositions associated with active thinking and learning. Let your pupils know when you are weighing up different options, tell them about difficult learning experiences you have had and try to relate what they are doing in lessons to real life as much as possible.
4   Try to make the lessons fun! Your pupils will very quickly pick up on your own attitudes, so if you appear excited and positive about the activities, there is a much greater chance that they will be too.

Question Nine

How should I get the programme started? Does it need any introduction?

It is recommended that you spend a short while explaining the purpose of this programme to the children. Explain that we learn about all sorts of interesting subjects at school and we learn how to use a variety of skills – both intellectual and physical. However, we rarely give enough time to considering what is possibly the most important skill of all: *how to use our brain.* You could point out that our brains are extraordinarily powerful and have incredible capacity – and yet they come with no instruction manual. Instead, we tend to stumble along, rather haphazardly working out how to use them. These lessons aim to fill in some of these 'brain instructions' by introducing the children to a variety of different thinking and learning skills and providing a range of tools and techniques to get the brain working in new ways.

You might want to use this introductory lesson to give each child a copy of the Thinking and Learning Skills folder cover provided on the CD Rom and talk through the stages of a typical lesson.

It is also a good idea to send a letter home to parents to keep them fully informed about your thinking and learning programme. Involving parents is vital and is discussed further in Chapter 7.

Question Ten

What about assessment? Can this programme help me to monitor how the thinking and learning skills of my pupils are developing?

Yes, it can. Copy the sheet 'Thinking and learning skills strategies and games' provided on pages 32–3 and on the CD Rom, as this provides a useful reminder of the strategies that are included in the programme. You may wish to highlight sections that you have covered and cross-refer to the 'THINK! skills overview' (page 31 and the CD Rom) to note the types of skills that your class has been working on. This will give you a useful guide to the terminology that could be included in your notes and reports for individual pupils.

It is likely that much of your evidence will be based on observation. One useful method is to keep a journal with a page devoted to each child, on which you can jot down notes during lessons. You could occasionally make audio or video recordings of individual groups, as this allows more time to reflect upon what your pupils' comments reveal about their thinking. The level and quality of interaction, discussion and ideas are often surprising and one particularly exciting aspect of the programme is that it allows pupils to shine in ways that might not otherwise have been discovered. Point this out when you notice it, as it can have a wonderful effect on morale for quieter, less confident pupils in particular, who might never have realised, for example, that they have a surprisingly rigorous and logical approach or that they are unusually quirky lateral thinkers.

A selection of pupil self-evaluation sheets ('Thinking about my thinking') is also included on the CD Rom. These are for occasional use with your class, as your pupils' own reflection and comments can add a valuable layer to your assessment.

What's the best way forward for me?

Shall I ...

- try to find ten minutes to spare at the beginning of each day to warm up with a thinking and learning skills activity from the 'Tune in!' section of the plans?

- make time to try out a selection of the THINK! lessons from across the programme?

- trial the complete set of seven THINK! lessons for my year group?

- schedule a weekly thinking and learning skills lesson into my timetable and use this for both the THINK! lessons and the follow-up curriculum ideas?

- look for further ways to adapt the THINK! strategies so that they suit the topics and subjects that my class is doing?

- use the whole lesson plans or shorten the sessions by selecting certain components or splitting them over two lessons?

- develop a thinking and learning skills approach across several year groups or a Key Stage?

- launch an integrated thinking and learning skills programme across the whole school, using these lessons as a starting point?

- run a thinking skills club at lunchtime using some of the ideas?

- hold an activity day with a thinking skills focus?

- lead a thinking and learning skills workshop in the holiday using a selection of the games and strategies?

Chapter 7

What could I do to take this further?

Continuing the programme

It is not possible to begin to 'cover' everything in one book, especially given that our understanding of thinking and learning is developing all the time. This programme offers a wide selection of approaches that can be effective in improving the quality of thinking and learning. Nevertheless, it is still very much a 'starter kit' and schools wishing to see a real change in abilities and behaviours are bound to want to take things further.

Ideally, schools are encouraged to follow up the lessons provided by developing their own curriculum applications and even their own techniques and ideas to incorporate into the THINK! structure. It is recommended that schools who are keen to engage in real change consider running weekly thinking skills lessons and using these to look in more depth at the different areas of skills.

Culture change

To bring about real and lasting change will often require a shift in a school's culture. While thinking and learning skills methods can be incorporated into the curriculum relatively easily, a great deal of time and commitment is required for the dispositions to become embedded in the ethos of the classroom or school. Key areas on which to focus include:

- Developing a shared vocabulary: ensure that all your staff are familiar with the thinking and learning skills and dispositions. Consider displaying the disposition words (cards are provided on the CD Rom) around the classrooms and in communal areas, so that everyone's familiarity with these is increased. Refer to these when praising pupils, rather than focusing solely on end results.
- Developing a shared approach: hold frequent staff discussions to gain consensus regarding the attitudes, values and teaching approach that are most likely to support this sort of programme (see tips under Question Eight on page 24.) and to evaluate and share experiences with using the techniques.
- Developing a shared agenda: ideally, try to make sure that everyone is involved in the programme and that all recognise its value. Look out for as many ways of reinforcing its messages as you can, for example by focusing on thinking and learning dispositions in assemblies, extra-curricular activities and assessment.

Support for teaching staff

For school-wide impact, time needs to be found for teachers to work together in small groups to think about the methods described and to develop the necessary curriculum opportunities and resources. Feedback situations could then be built into your staff meetings, so that teachers have a chance to comment on which strategies worked particularly well and which might be better suited to alternative year groups or curriculum contexts. Even with the best will in the world, it takes time to think of new ideas and the success of the programme is likely to be greatly enhanced if teachers are supported in initiating changes in practice.

Involving parents

Teaching thinking and learning skills is so important – and has received such attention in the media – that parents are likely to be excited and enthusiastic about your school's work in this area. Involve them as much as possible: after all, your pupils spend a tiny fraction of their time at school and what happens at home can play a significant part in children's development. As suggested previously (see Question Nine in Chapter 6), it is worth sending a letter home to parents to explain the approach that your school has decided to take. Alongside this, you may also wish to:

- Formalise the 'Keep thinking' tasks, or invent your own, so that your pupils take these home and carry them out with the involvement of their parents
- Make a leaflet to describe what your school is doing to support the development of the pupils' thinking and learning skills
- Ensure that parents' evenings and pupil reports make reference to the pupils' thinking and learning skills and dispositions
- Describe some of the lessons you are doing in bulletins that go home to parents or on the school website
- Hold a special event for parents, offering them the chance to visit several classes and see thinking and learning skills lessons in practice
- Give your parents regular opportunities to feed back with their views about the programme

Widening the impact

If you want to take things further still, why not consider extending the programme by setting up thinking skills clubs and holiday workshops? Thinking and learning skills workshops, for instance, are ideally suited to more able pupils, but can be opened to all abilities should you prefer. Simply pick out some of the activities and games from this book and apply them to an overall theme for your workshop.

Further resources

Many of the lesson plans refer to books and websites that support the particular theories and tools that are used. These contain a wealth of ideas that will be of great value to anyone who is keen to pursue a deeper understanding of the thinking and learning field.

Part Two

The THINK! Programme

Overview documents

Lesson plans and resources

THINK! skills overview

This diagram shows the component skills within each of the seven key areas:

1. Metacognition
2. Questioning
3. Information skills
4. Critical thinking
5. Creative thinking
6. Decision making
7. Memory skills

In its centre are the thinking and learning habits or dispositions that should be encouraged at every opportunity throughout the programme.

The skills developed within the missing strand – Communication – are detailed in the table entitled 'Heads Together: Development of Skills'.

 A full-colour version of this diagram is provided on the CD Rom.

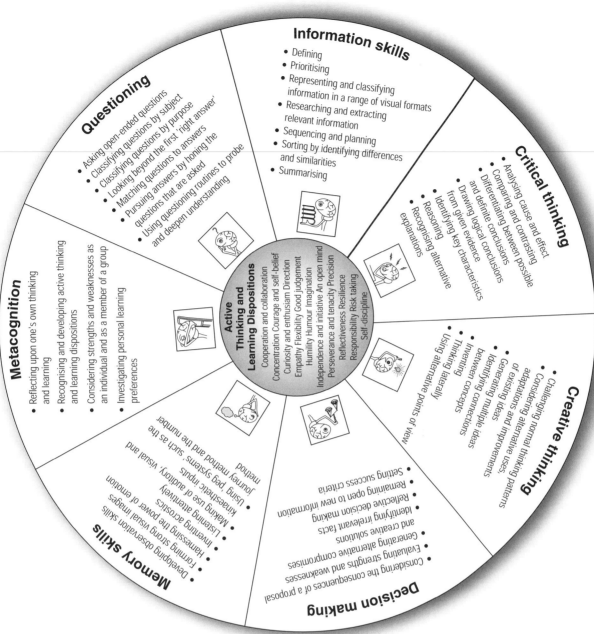

Questioning
- Asking open-ended questions
- Classifying questions by subject
- Classifying questions by purpose
- Looking beyond the first 'right answer'
- Matching questions to answers
- Pursuing answers by honing the questions that are asked
- Using questioning routines to probe and deepen understanding

Information skills
- Defining
- Prioritising
- Representing and classifying information in a range of visual formats
- Researching and extracting relevant information
- Sequencing and planning
- Sorting by identifying differences and similarities
- Summarising

Critical thinking
- Analysing cause and effect
- Comparing and contrasting
- Differentiating between possible and definite conclusions
- Drawing logical conclusions from given evidence
- Identifying key characteristics
- Reasoning
- Recognising alternative explanations

Creative thinking
- Challenging normal thinking patterns
- Considering alternative uses for, adaptations and improvements of existing
- Generating ideas
- Identifying multiple ideas
- Inventing concepts
- Thinking – Identifying connections between concepts
- Thinking laterally
- Using alternative points of view

Decision making
- Considering the consequences of a proposal
- Evaluating strengths and weaknesses
- Generating alternative compromises and creative solutions
- Identifying irrelevant facts
- Reflective decision making
- Remaining open to new information
- Setting success criteria

Memory skills
- Developing observation skills
- Forming strong visual images
- Harnessing the power of emotion
- Inventing acrostics
- Listening attentively
- Making use of auditory, visual and kinaesthetic inputs
- Using 'peg systems' such as the journey method and the number method

Metacognition
- Reflecting upon one's own thinking and learning
- Recognising and developing active thinking and learning dispositions
- Considering strengths and weaknesses as an individual and as a member of a group
- Investigating personal learning preferences

Active Thinking and Learning Dispositions
Cooperation and collaboration
Concentration Courage and self-belief
Curiosity and enthusiasm Direction
Empathy Flexibility Good judgement
Humility Humour Imagination
Independence and initiative An open mind
Perseverance and tenacity Precision
Reflectiveness Resilience
Responsibility Risk taking
Self-discipline

Thinking and learning skills strategies and games: a complete list

Strand	Strategy	Year group	Also suitable for ...
METACOGNITION	What's in my head?	1	-
	Learning about thinking	1	2
	First to Find ...	2	3
	Thinking about learning	2	3
	I'm good at ...	3	2, 4
	A Recipe for Good Thinking and Learning	3	4, 5
	Active Thinking and Learning	4	5, 6
	Freeze Frame	4	5, 6
	My Amazing Brain	5	4, 6
	Learning Styles	5	4, 6
	Re-visiting the dispositions	6	5
	Disposition Action Plans	6	5
QUESTIONING	Star Questions	1	2
	Questioning for Understanding	1	2, 3, 4, 5, 6
	Three 'Whys' Men	2	2, 3
	What do you wonder?	2	2, 3, 4, 5, 6
	Twenty Questions	3	2, 4, 5, 6
	Asking 'Thinking' Questions	3	4, 5, 6
	What if?	4	2, 3, 5, 6
	Things you never knew about ...	4	5, 6
	Catch me if you can!	5	6
	What's the question?	5	1, 2, 3, 4, 6
	Tell me the truth	6	1, 2, 3, 4, 5
	The Question Ladder	6	5
INFORMATION SKILLS	Mix 'n' Match	1	2, 3, 4
	Odd One Out	1	2, 3, 4, 5, 6
	Six Steps to Success	2	3, 4
	Flow diagrams	2	1, 3, 4, 5, 6
	Tree Diagram Challenge	3	4, 5, 6
	Visual Mapping	3	1, 2, 4, 5, 6
	Mystery Word	4	3, 5, 6
	Diamond Ranking	4	2, 3, 5, 6
	Word Links	5	4, 6
	Be a Thinking Detective!	5	4, 6
	What's it all about?	6	4, 5
	Yes/No Tree Diagrams	6	3, 4, 5
CRITICAL THINKING	What am I?	1	2, 3
	Patchwork Thinking	1	2, 3, 4, 5, 6
	Tied Up in Knots!	2	3
	Categories of Comparison	2	3, 4, 5, 6
	Su Doku puzzles	3	2, 4, 5, 6
	Define it!	3	4, 5, 6
	Picture this!	4	2, 3, 5, 6
	Alternative Explanations	4	3, 5, 6
	Disconnect!	5	4, 6
	Cause and Effect: Multi-Flow Maps	5	2, 3, 4, 6
	Amazing but true!	6	4, 5
	Layers of Inference	6	3, 4, 5

Strand	Strategy	Year group	Also suitable for...
CREATIVE THINKING	Start with a Squiggle	1	2, 3, 4, 5, 6
	Use it or lose it!	1	2, 3, 4, 5, 6
	Connect!	2	3, 4, 5, 6
	Concept Collages	2	3, 4, 5, 6
	Reverse Thinking	3	2, 4, 5, 6
	Lateral Links	3	2, 4, 5, 6
	Switch!	4	5, 6
	Points of View	4	1, 2, 3, 5, 6
	The Problem Game	5	1, 2, 3, 4, 6
	Improve it!	5	4, 6
	Absurd Analogies	6	4, 5
	Random Input method	6	3, 4, 5
DECISION MAKING	Stumped!	1	2, 3, 4, 5, 6
	Target Board	1	2, 3,4, 5, 6
	Imagine that ...	2	1, 3, 4, 5, 6
	Weighing Up the Options	2	3, 4, 5, 6
	Hidden Hypotheticals	3	2, 4, 5, 6
	Consider the Consequences	3	4, 5, 6
	Think 'n' Run	4	2, 3, 5, 6
	Mysteries: Detective!	4	1, 2, 3, 5, 6
	What could it be?	5	1, 2, 3, 4, 6
	Reflective Decision Making	5	4, 6
	Up in the Air	6	2, 3, 4, 5
	Opening Up the Options	6	5
MEMORY SKILLS	Mystery Voices	1	2, 3, 4, 5, 6
	All Ears!	1	2, 3, 4, 5, 6
	Spot the Difference	2	1, 3, 4, 5, 6
	Memory Pictures	2	3, 4, 5, 6
	The Acrostic Game	3	4, 5, 6
	Visual Images	3	2, 4, 5, 6
	Look, Speak, Act!	4	3, 5, 6
	The Story Method	4	1, 2, 3, 5, 6
	Break up!	5	3, 4, 6
	The Journey Method	5	2, 3, 4, 6
	It's a mad world!	6	2, 3, 4, 5
	Number Hooks	6	5

'Heads together': development of skills

The table below shows how a series of communication skills can be developed gradually through use of the 'Heads together' discussions.

	Lesson 1 Metacognition	Lesson 2 Questioning	Lesson 3 Information skills	Lesson 4 Critical thinking	Lesson 5 Creative thinking	Lesson 6 Decision making	Lesson 7 Memory skills
Y1	Set rules	Being brave with ideas		Listening carefully to others		Giving reasons for opinions	
Y2	Set rules	Giving reasons for opinions		Expressing agreement		Expressing disagreement	
Y3	Set rules	Expressing agreement and disagreement		Taking a 'thinking moment'		Explaining ideas clearly	
Y4	Set rules	Clarifying and asking for clarification		Giving examples		Asking relevant questions	
Y5	Set rules	Quoting or paraphrasing what others have said		Building on what others have said		Being concise – avoiding diversion	
Y6	Set rules	Challenging others to give reasons or examples		Differentiating between fact and opinion		Using persuasive language	

Year 1

Lesson plans and resources

Year 1   Lesson 1

Resources

Activity Sheet: enlarged copy of **My Magical Thinking Potion**
Teacher instructions: **The Good Thinker Game**
Activity cards: one set of **The Good Thinker Game Cards**
20 Dispositions of an Active Thinker and Learner
Good Thinker Certificates
You will need to find: A soft toy, to be named 'Brains'

Tune in!   D C   Activity: What's in my head?

- Tell your pupils they are going to learn about some of the types of thinking that our amazing brains can do. Explain that thinking is often private – it happens secretly in our heads and no one else can know exactly what we're thinking about – but it's important to talk about it so we make sure we're using our brains really well.
- Invite your class to guess what you're thinking. After a few guesses, reveal the answer by completing the sentence, 'Inside my head, I am thinking about …'
- With your pupils in a circle, ask them to take turns to step forward and say, 'Inside _____'s head, he/she was thinking about … *(repeating what the previous person said)* Inside my head, I am thinking of …' Try to keep the pace fast.

Heads together

'Heads together' Introductory session   Page 146

Investigate   D C   Thinking and Learning Tool: Learning about thinking

- Introduce Brains, your soft toy, who is coming to these lessons because he's a really good thinker.
- Explain that not everyone knows what a good thinker is or has the confidence to believe they can be good at thinking, so you're going to create a magical potion, full of good thinking ingredients, to remind everyone of what's needed to become good thinkers like Brains.
- Display an enlarged copy of the sheet 'My Magical Thinking Potion'. Pretend to ask Brains to help get you started by suggesting 3 ingredients:

  o Ideas – good thinkers need to be prepared to come up with lots of ideas
  o Courage – good thinkers are brave and share their ideas and thoughts
  o Mistakes – good thinkers know that mistakes are important as this is often the way you do your best learning

- Discuss each of these and add them to the picture. Ask your pupils for their own ideas.
- Follow the instructions provided to play the 'Good Thinker' game.

The type of ingredients you're hoping to include are simpler versions of the ideas listed on the sheet '20 Dispositions of an Active Thinker and Learner', e.g.:

- Questions – good thinkers are curious and ask questions about the world
- Effort – good thinkers keep trying and don't give up when things feel hard

Find a way of linking all your pupils' ideas to the discussion at hand. Emphasise the fact that everyone can learn to be a better thinker, no matter how old they are or how clever they feel.

Now reflect!

Questions to consider could include:

- What have we learnt about good thinkers?
- In what ways are you a good thinker? (Your pupils could take it in turns to say something positive about themselves, completing the sentence: 'I am a good thinker because I ...)
- How could you be a better thinker? What are you going to try to do?

Keep thinking

Make a copy of the class's good thinking potion and send this home so that families can see and discuss the type of attitudes and habits that you hope to encourage. Further ideas can be brought in and added to the display.

Follow-up ideas

Unlike the following six lessons, there is no curriculum follow-up for the 'Habits' lesson. However, you may still like to try some of the following:

- Talk about the importance of exercise for our bodies and use this as a way of introducing a discussion about how to exercise our brains. Ask your pupils for their ideas. Ian Gilbert explains, 'To grow your brain, give it the equivalent of a full regular workout – feed it with information through all the senses. See new sights, taste new tastes, smell new smells, feel new ... feels.' You might like to keep a wall chart to record 'New things we've noticed today'.
- Involve Brains in lessons wherever possible. He could be asked to offer advice when pupils are stuck and to give suggestions and ideas. Challenge your class to read his mind when they're faced with a particular situation, encouraging them to put themselves in the position of a 'good thinker' and come up with the ideas themselves.
- To reinforce the dispositions, play the 'Good Thinker Game' again, giving different cards to different pupils.
- Use the 'Good Thinker Certificates' to reward pupils for displaying the sort of traits discussed.

Suggestions for display

Make a large picture of a cauldron, with the pupils' ideas on individually named 'think clouds' above it. Refer to these during other lessons and discussions.

Further resources

There are many excellent resources to support the development of positive thinking and learning habits. See Chapter 6 in Part One for a list of recommended books and websites.

For a highly original approach to thinking about thinking try: *Little Owl's Book of Thinking* by Ian Gilbert (2004), Carmarthen: Crown House Publishing.

Resources

Poster: enlarged copy of **Star Questions**
Activity sheet: individual copies of **Star Questions about ...**
Poster: enlarged copy of **Questioning for Understanding**
Activity sheet: one copy between two of the **Questioning for Understanding picture sheet**
Teacher instructions: **Questioning for Understanding sample dialogues**
You will need to find: your class's soft toy, Brains

Tune in!   D C   Activity: Star Questions

- Ask your class to recall ways in which Brains is a good thinker. Remind them that asking questions is an important thinking ingredient, as good thinkers are curious about the world around them and want to understand it.
- With your pupils standing in a circle, show them the poster 'Star Questions' and read the 6 question words. Invite someone to volunteer to stand in the middle.
- Taking it in turns, the first 6 pupils jump forward, clap and call out a question about the volunteer. Each should begin with a different starter word from the star. The person in the middle should try to answer the questions.
- After 6 questions, the seventh person takes over in the middle. Try to keep the pace fast.

Heads together

This lesson:	Philosophy for Children, 'Generating the Question Session'	Page 150
Curriculum lesson:	Philosophy for Children, 'Discussion Session'	Page 151
Discussion skill:	Being brave with ideas. Encourage your class to speak up, to have confidence and to share their thoughts without fearing others' response	

Investigate   D C   Thinking and Learning Tool: Questioning for Understanding

- Explain that Brains has discovered that some questions are particularly useful in helping him understand and find out about things. This activity teaches one of his favourite questioning routines.
- Display the sheet 'Questioning for Understanding' and read out the 3 question steps.
- Give out copies of the first photograph and ask your pupils to look closely at it as there are all sorts of things that they might notice. Begin by giving an example, e.g. 'I notice that ... it's someone's birthday'. Can anyone explain how you knew this was true?
- What else do your pupils notice? Where appropriate, follow up their comments with one or both of the other questions. The sample dialogues show how to probe for further evidence and reasoning. If a child is unsure about how to answer, open the question up to everyone.
- Repeat with the second picture.
- Praise everyone for their good thinking and point out how much more they discovered about the pictures by using this routine than if they had simply looked at it normally.

For this activity, you may prefer to ask each child in turn or simply allow pupils to put forward ideas as and when they have them.

Now reflect!

Questions to consider could include:

- Why is asking questions something that good thinkers like to do?
- Can you think of any times when it's particularly important to ask questions?
- What other things in the classroom could we use for our 'Questioning for Understanding' routine?

Keep thinking

Invite your pupils to choose any topic, e.g. dinosaurs or outer space, and think of 6 interesting 'Star Questions' about it. Record these using the 'Star Questions about …' sheet. Photocopy onto thin card, so they can be rotated when displayed with a drawing pin through the centre.

Follow-up ideas

Curriculum-based lesson

'Star Questions' helps pupils begin to explore almost any new subject and encourages them to direct the course of their own learning. Introduce your topic by inviting the class to think of 6 'Star Questions' they'd like to ask. At the end of the topic, your pupils can check whether they've answered all their original questions.

The 'Questioning for Understanding' routine is excellent for encouraging observation skills and a deeper level of thinking. For example, it could be used in:

- English – to talk about a short story, nursery rhyme or poem.
- History/Religious Studies – to investigate an artefact.
- Art – to learn to explore a painting.
- Geography – to discuss a photograph of a scene from another country.

Suggestions for display

 Display the class's 'Star Questions' about a new topic and add answers, in the form of pictures or simple statements, whenever these are found.

Notes for use by other year groups

While 'Star Questions' is designed to introduce younger pupils to questioning and is replaced by 'Asking Thinking Questions' in Year 3, the 'Questioning for Understanding' routine can be used at any level and across the whole curriculum. For instance, use it to:

- explore a passage from a class novel
- analyse a scientific experiment
- generate ideas about a picture of a geographical phenomenon such as a volcano

By experiencing this sort of routine frequently at school, your pupils will learn to support their observations automatically with explanations and hypotheses. Extend this with older pupils by developing other questioning routines and getting more able pupils to invent versions of their own.

Further resources

This routine was adapted from ideas developed by Project Zero, a research and development group at the Harvard Graduate School of Education. Further examples can be found on their 'Visible Thinking' website at:
 www.pz.harvard.edu/vt/VisibleThinking_html_files/01_VisibleThinkingInAction/01a_VTInAction.html.

Resources

Activity cards: one set of 3 **Odd One Out cards** per group
You will need to find: your class's soft toy, Brains, and a set of 5 everyday items

Tune in!   D   C   Activity: Mix 'n' Match

- Seat pupils around 5 objects previously sorted into 2 groups, e.g. by shape, colour, size, use or particular features.
- Explain that Brains has 2 groups of objects, but doesn't know how they've been sorted. Can the class help? Use the discussion to consider and clarify common classification methods.
- Ask a volunteer to sort the objects in a different way and secretly tell you their method. If appropriate, make this more challenging by insisting on one pile of 3 and one of 2 items. Can the class guess how the volunteer was thinking? Gather suggestions and ask the volunteer to reveal whether anyone was right.
- Repeat with further volunteers.
- Discuss which method your pupils liked best. Point out the skills they used, such as imagination, sorting and finding differences and similarities, and explain that these will help them in the main activity.

Heads together

This lesson:	Philosophy for Children, 'Generating the Question Session'	Page 150
Curriculum lesson:	Philosophy for Children, 'Discussion Session'	Page 151
Discussion skill:	Being brave with ideas. Encourage your class to speak up, to have confidence and to share their thoughts without fearing others' response	

Investigate   D   G3   Thinking and Learning Tool: Odd One Out

- Hold up one of the sets of 3 cards provided and invite your pupils to suggest which could be the odd one out, supporting their answers with clear reasons.
- Give each group a set of 3 pictures. Pupils take it in turns to complete the sentence, 'I think .... is the odd one out because ....'. Emphasise the importance of listening to each other.
- Monitor groups closely to ensure everyone is included. Offer specific praise, e.g. by commenting when a particularly unusual, creative or interesting idea is put forward.
- Afterwards, ask each group to show their cards and to share their most interesting sorting methods. Other pupils could suggest alternative methods as well.

Helpful Hints

Children will often sort objects in ways that are not logical, in which case ask questions such as:

- Why have you placed this object in a separate group?
- Does that reason help us understand why this object is different to the others?
- How does that object fit with the other two? What's the same about them?

If the class find this too challenging, ask for a volunteer who thinks they could sort the objects by colour, then for someone to sort them by size etc. Each time, ask the rest of the class to explain the volunteer's method in more detail.

Now reflect!

Questions to consider could include:

- How did you find this activity?
- What have you learnt about your thinking?
- Can you think of any other situations where you might want to choose the odd one out?

Keep thinking

Suggest that your pupils make up their own Odd One Out games. Set a homework task to complete with parental help, to record as many different ways as possible of finding the odd one out with a set of 3 objects found at home.

Follow-up ideas

Curriculum-based lesson

The Odd One Out tool promotes flexibility of thought and creativity, requiring pupils to think beyond the first 'right answer' and to analyse information in different ways. It can deepen understanding of a variety of curriculum subjects. Create further sets of picture cards or objects linked with a particular topic or subject, then follow the same approach. For example:

- Mathematics – finding the odd one out when given 3 numbers can help to clarify understanding of simple number properties, e.g. odd and even numbers; using two- or three-dimensional shapes can lead to useful observations about their properties.
- English – consider 3 characters from a familiar story, e.g. Little Red Riding Hood.
- Science – use 3 pictures or samples of different types of food; gather real objects made of various materials, so that properties (whether they are sharp, soft, rough, smooth, waterproof etc.) and uses (whether they are used for cooking, writing, sport etc.) can be considered.
- Humanities – make sets of artefacts linked to History, Geography or Religious Studies topics.

Suggestions for display

✂ Display the cards, surrounded by different suggestions in speech bubbles.

✂ Mount pictures of 3 items at the beginning of each week on an 'Odd One Out' board and ask pupils to come up with as many ideas as they can. Record ideas in empty 'ideas bubbles' on the display. Pupils could vote for the most creative idea at the end of the week.

Notes for use by other year groups

Introduce the Odd One Out activity with older pupils by playing the 'Mix 'n' Match' game as a competition. Ask teams of pupils to find 5 objects and challenge them to sort these into 2 groups – one of 2 and one of 3 items. Each time a team thinks of a method, check their reasoning and get them to note its name. Award 1 point for each method, with bonus marks for any really creative ideas. Afterwards, ask your pupils which method was their most interesting. Point out that first ideas are rarely best ideas and that the more unusual, creative suggestions tend to take more time.

Give older pupils Odd One Out cards representing more advanced topics, e.g. 3 historical characters, 3 photographs of the same event, 3 advertisements or Letters to the Editor from a newspaper, or 3 paintings or sculptures by a particular artist.

Lesson 4

Resources

Teacher instructions: **What am I?**
Activity cards: group sets of the **What am I? cards**
Activity sheet: **Patchwork Thinking** (curriculum follow-up)
You will need to find: your class's soft toy, Brains, and one mystery object from the classroom

Tune In!　D　G3　Activity: What am I?

- Choose a mystery object for Brains to hide and explain that he wants your pupils to guess what this is from just 3 clues. Relay these to the class – each beginning with 'I am something ...'. For instance, clues for an egg box might be 'I am something that holds things', 'I am something that is made of cardboard' and 'I am something that is a very unusual shape'.
- Invite possible answers and use these to discuss how the pupils are making use of the clues.
- Once they have worked out the object, ask how your 3 clues could have been improved.
- Play the 'What am I?' game, following the instructions provided.
- Afterwards, ask the class what they thought of the game. How did they come up with the clues?

Heads together

This lesson: 　　　　Philosophy for Children, 'Generating the Question Session' 　　Page 150
Curriculum lesson: 　Philosophy for Children, 'Discussion Session' 　　　　　　　Page 151
Discussion skill: 　　Listening carefully to others. Encourage your pupils to develop good listening behaviours: to face the person who is talking, to concentrate on what they are saying and to wait until they have finished before speaking.

Investigate　　G3　　Thinking and Learning Tool: Patchwork Thinking

- Explain that this game requires your pupils to think in different ways: to be creative (have lots of unusual ideas), logical (think very carefully and give reasons) and able to make decisions together.
- Ask 2 volunteers to choose a 'What am I?' card each and invite the class to suggest ways in which the items are similar. Accept several answers, then repeat with 2 more cards.
- Give each group a full set of 16 cards and ask them to lay out the cards face up in a 4 by 4 'patchwork'.
- First challenge: arrange the cards so that each one is similar in some way to the cards on its left and right. Allow sufficient time for this and check everyone understands the task.
- Second challenge: arrange the cards so that each is linked not only with those to its left and right, but also with the cards above and below it.
- Third challenge (for more able pupils): arrange the cards so that they are logically linked with the cards that touch their corners as well.

During the activity, check your pupils' thinking by circulating between groups, picking out 2 cards that are touching and challenging them to explain the reasoning behind the link. Emphasise at all stages that groups must be able to give clear reasons for their decisions.

Now reflect!

Questions to consider could include:

- Which was your favourite linking idea? How imaginative (out of 5) was it?
- Which were the hardest two cards to link?
- What sort of thinking were you doing for these activities?

Keep thinking

Invite your pupils to invent 'What am I?' clues for objects of their choice. Write these on large cards, display them and use them as a daily challenge for the other pupils in the class. The mystery object could be revealed at the end of the day.

Follow-up ideas

Curriculum-based lesson

Use 'What am I?' within the curriculum by making cards with pictures of mathematical shapes, scientific equipment, historical artefacts, places of worship or characters from favourite books. This game helps children to become familiar with key vocabulary, as they must think hard to generate alternative ways of describing the items.

'Patchwork Thinking' is a very useful tool within lessons. Use an enlarged copy of the sheet 'Patchwork Thinking' and give out 16 words or pictures relating to a range of subjects, e.g.:

- English – select components (locations, emotions, pictures of objects or characters etc.) of a story that is familiar to the class.
- Mathematics – use a selection of numbers and two- and three-dimensional shapes.
- Religious Studies – use words or pictures from a particular religious story or parable.
- Science/History/Geography – pick key words or pictures from your current topic.

Suggestions for display

Create and display large-scale patchworks. Each day, your pupils can move the pieces around, so that new links are discovered and explained.

Notes for use by other year groups

With older pupils, begin with a game of 'What am I?', though with the challenge that they must come up with just one clue that represents the most important characteristic of that object.

Use the main activity as a revision exercise, asking your pupils to generate 16 words themselves from their current topic. Alternatively, begin by presenting them with a piece of text and ask them to pick out the 16 most important words to use. Another option is for pairs of pupils to be given a copy of the sheet 'Patchwork Thinking', containing words, pictures or a combination of the two. Each player takes it in turns to identify a square, colour it with their own colour and explain how it links to those around it. For each logical link, they are awarded a point. This is a good revision tool as it encourages a deeper understanding of interrelated concepts.

Further resources

Thanks to Mike Fleetham for permission to use Patchwork Thinking.
Visit www.thinkingclassroom.co.uk for more free Thinking Skills resources.

Year 1

Lesson 5

Resources

Teacher instructions: **Start with a Squiggle**
Activity sheet: **Use it or lose it!** (for more able/older pupils)
You will need to find: your class's soft toy, Brains, and a set of hula hoops

Tune in!　　D　C　　　　　Activity: Start with a Squiggle!

- Tell your class that Brains wants to find out how creative they can be. Choose a shape from the sheet 'Start with a Squiggle' and draw it on the board. What could it be?
- Accept a few answers, then prompt further ideas by inviting your pupils to imagine it from different view points: above them, below them and straight ahead.
- Praise your class for their imaginative ideas.

Heads together

This lesson: Philosophy for Children, 'Generating the Question Session'   Page 150
Curriculum lesson: Philosophy for Children, 'Discussion Session'   Page 151
Discussion skill: Listening carefully to others. Encourage your pupils to develop good listening behaviours: to face the person who is talking, to concentrate on what they are saying and to wait until they have finished before speaking.

Investigate　　D　G2　　　Thinking and Learning Tool: Use it or lose it!

- Explain that one of Brains's favourite creative thinking activities is to think about how everyday objects can be used in different ways.
- Give each pair of pupils a hula hoop and ask them to describe it. List its properties on the board, e.g. it is plastic/round/hard; it can be bent into different shapes; it's big enough to climb through etc.
- Ask them what we normally use hula hoops for and relate their ideas to the properties listed.
- Tell your pupils they are going to come up with as many ways of using a hula hoop as they can. Emphasise the need to consider the properties listed and think about *entirely new* ways of using the hoop that might be fun or useful.
- Allow some quiet thinking time first, then get your pupils to work in pairs to develop further ideas. You could move to a larger room or hall to allow them to try these out. Point out that the best creative thinkers will realise their hula hoops can be used for many things apart from games. They may, for instance, invent ways in which the hoops could be useful in the classroom, at home or in the garden.
- Invite each pupil to choose their favourite idea and tell this to the class. Value all ideas, so they develop confidence and learn to appreciate all suggestions, however unusual they sound.

With older children, it takes effort to develop the sort of culture where no one puts down another idea and everyone feels comfortable in making suggestions, so it's worth beginning to build these traits at an early age. This does not mean insisting that no one should laugh at another person's idea: you are trying to develop robust, confident children who can see the funny side of their own and other people's ideas, while at the same time being able and willing to scrutinise even the most ridiculous suggestion in case it prompts something new or useful.

Now reflect!

Questions to consider could include:

- How can you spot a good creative thinker?
- How creative do you think you are?
- In what other situations might it be useful to come up with lots of possible ideas before picking the best one?

Keep thinking

Ask your class how many uses they can think of for a paper clip. You could set this type of activity as a weekly challenge, with a prize for the person who thinks of the most different possibilities.

Follow-up ideas

Curriculum-based lesson

Too often – and especially as they get older – pupils are content with the first seemingly good idea or answer they come across, so the purpose of this activity is to practise the initial 'generating ideas' stage, so that it becomes second nature. Encourage lots of unusual, inventive thoughts, then get your pupils to select their best one and present it in some way, perhaps verbally or as a picture. Look for a curriculum context where there are few, if any, 'wrong' answers, e.g.:

- English – focus on a dilemma from a favourite story, e.g. how many ways can you think of for Little Red Riding Hood to beat the wolf?
- Geography – how many routes can you find from here to the hall? Make a class map
- Design and Technology – how many uses can you find for a cardboard tube/balloon/cotton reel?

Suggestions for display

When displaying work, make explicit the *processes* involved in the activity as well as the end results, by clarifying the two main stages of thinking: (a) idea generation (and its associated creative thinking skills: imagination, open-mindedness, flexibility etc.) then (b) selection (and its associated skills: comparing, sorting, decision making etc.)

Notes for use by other year groups

'Start with a Squiggle' is popular with all ages and is a great way of countering the fear of getting the answer wrong and looking silly, which can act as such a barrier to creativity for older children.

Finding multiple uses for everyday objects such as a coat hanger, a matchbox, a skateboard or a ping pong ball fits well within a Design and Technology curriculum, generates extremely creative ideas and can be linked with a topic on recycling. The sheet 'Use it or lose it!' requires pupils to consider the characteristics of the object before drawing on this to produce a list of alternative uses.

In other subjects, focus on generating multiple *theories* or *suggestions* so a range of answers can be assessed and evaluated, e.g. in Geography ask pupils how many different ways they can come up with to take care of the school environment, and in Science how many ideas they can think of to explain why rainbows exist. Then, instead of simply selecting one best suggestion, older pupils could present *all* their theories on a spectrum, from the least to the most likely. This emphasises the importance of considering a wide range of ideas rather than focusing on a single 'correct' one.

Resources

Activity sheet: an enlarged copy of **Target Board ... perfect pet**
Activity cards: a set of the **Target Board picture cards**
Activity sheet: **Target Board** (curriculum follow-up)
You will need to find: your class's soft toy, Brains

Tune in!   D C   Activity: Stumped!

- Tell your class that it's Brains's birthday, but he can't decide how to celebrate it. He knows he shouldn't just make a quick decision, so wants them to help by listing all the options.
- Take turns around a circle to come up with as many suggestions as possible. If a pupil chooses to 'pass', return to them later.
- Each pupil should choose their favourite idea, giving a reason for this choice. Point out that different people may make different decisions, but the important thing is to consider all the possibilities first.

Heads together

This lesson: Philosophy for Children, 'Generating the Question Session'   Page 150
Curriculum lesson: Philosophy for Children, 'Discussion Session'   Page 151
Discussion skill: Giving reasons for opinions. Encourage your pupils to support their statements with clear reasons and examples, using 'because ...'

Investigate   C G3   Thinking and Learning Tool: Target Board

- Explain that Brains has to decide which pet to get for his birthday and wants to show your pupils a new method for making decisions like this.
- What makes a perfect pet? Share and record ideas, then use voting and discussion to narrow down a list of 5 'rules', e.g. 'My perfect pet should play with me', 'My perfect pet should be friendly' and 'My perfect pet should be easy to look after'.
- Display an enlarged copy of the 'Target Board' sheet. Invite a volunteer to put their finger inside the outer circle of the target board.
- Hold up an animal picture from the set of cards. Read out the first rule and decide together whether the animal passes this 'test'. If so, the volunteer moves their finger inwards one place to the next circle.
- Repeat this process for each rule, the volunteer moving their finger inwards one layer for an affirmative answer and keeping their finger stationary if the test isn't passed. After considering all 5 criteria, write the animal's name or attach its smaller picture on the diagram to show which layer it reached. Repeat for all 6 animals.
- How can the target board help your pupils decide which of the animals 'did the best'? Discuss which animal they chose by this method – was it the one they might have expected? Can they think of a different animal that would do even better?

More able children may understand that the 'rules' represent *criteria* against which various options can be judged. It should be emphasised that, by thinking about these criteria, they are more likely to make decisions that are fair and consistent.

Now reflect!

Questions to consider could include:

- What did 'Stumped!' and 'Target Board' teach you about how good thinkers make important decisions?
- Can you think of any other decisions where the Target Board method could be used?

Keep thinking

Set the class another similar task by asking them to think about which 5 questions they would ask to decide: What makes a good friend? What makes a happy classroom or school?

Follow-up ideas

Curriculum-based lesson

The 'Target Board' tool can apply to a range of curriculum or topic areas, for example:

- Science – considering which seed is likely to grow the best, by checking whether it has all the necessary conditions such as water, soil, light, warmth etc.; or assessing the value of a range of meals by looking at the balance of ingredients, food types, taste etc.
- English – deciding which fairy tale hits the bull's eye.
- Art – judging a selection of paintings by a given artist or within a particular movement.
- Geography – selecting the best place for a picnic, a holiday or a class outing.

Suggestions for display

✂ Display an enlarged Target Board with pictures of the animals placed on it and a list of the chosen criteria. Add questions such as 'Would you have chosen the same rules as we did?' and 'Can you work out how the tortoise ended up where it did?' Include further animal pictures to be placed on the Target Board.

Notes for use by other year groups

'Stumped!' can be used with older pupils to address:

- Silly situations (such as 'You're stuck up a tree! What could you do?' and 'Your bucket has a hole in it! What could you do?')
- Moral dilemmas or issues that may have arisen in the class, relating for example to friendship problems (Your best friend won't talk to you. What could you do?)
- Strategies for effective revision (You're finding it hard to concentrate. What could you do?)

Follow up by asking which was the most unusual/creative/sensible/dangerous solution etc.

Older pupils can decide independently on a list of criteria to use with the Target Board. Use the smaller animal picture cards with groups or investigate which television programme, sports car, holiday or pop star hits the bull's eye. Curriculum examples could include:

- History – judge the effectiveness of different Tudor monarchs or compare the usefulness of a range of historical sources to determine what happened during a particular event.
- English – weigh up which story, chapter, play or poem is the 'best' one.
- Technology – evaluate board-games, puppets or bridges or consider the suitability of a range of materials for a given purpose.

Alternatively, use the Target Board for self-assessment. Decide together on criteria by which work in a particular subject will be judged, then keep the sheet in the front of exercise books to refer to.

Further resources

The 'Target Board' tool was developed by Anne De A'Echeverria of the Northumberland Thinking for Learning Unit. Further examples of its use can be found in the article 'On target for transfer' in Issue 17 of the magazine *Teaching Thinking and Creativity* (Autumn 2005, pp 12–19).

Resources

Teacher instructions: **All Ears !**
Activity sheet: individual copies of **All Ears !**
You will need to find: your class's soft toy, Brains

Tune In! [D] [C]   Activity: Mystery Voices

- Select a volunteer to stand facing away from the other pupils. The others should gather behind that pupil, so he or she doesn't know where each person is standing.
- Point silently to a pupil and ask him or her to say 'Hello … *(child's name)*… How are you?' in a disguised voice.
- The pupil at the front has 3 attempts to guess who was speaking. If they are correct, increase the challenge by choosing 2 people to speak together with disguised voices. If the person at the front guesses this correctly again, they become a Listening Champion and you can pick someone else to take over. If the person guesses incorrectly 3 times, the mystery voice has 'won' and takes over at the front.

Heads together

This lesson: Philosophy for Children, 'Generating the Question Session'   Page 150
Curriculum lesson: Philosophy for Children, 'Discussion Session'   Page 151
Discussion skill: Giving reasons for opinions. Encourage your pupils to support their
                      statements with clear reasons and examples, using 'because …'

Investigate [C] [G3]   Thinking and Learning Tool: All Ears!

- Tell your class that Brains has made up a game to help them practise their listening skills.
- Explain the rules:
  - The pupils follow a set of instructions to draw a picture
  - Each instruction is given once and not repeated
  - While the instruction is read out, they must sit on their hands!
- Give pupils the sheet 'All Ears!' and check everyone has the equipment listed on the teacher instruction sheet.
- Read out the first instruction and give your pupils time to respond. You may need to help them with the meaning of 'right' and 'left'.
- When everyone has finished, repeat the instruction and draw the answer on the board. Pupils who have done this correctly can record a mark in the 'My score' box. Award no half marks for being nearly right!
- Repeat with each of the instructions on the sheet.
- Complete by discussing how pupils felt about the activity and noting this in the 'How did I do?' part of the sheet.

Poor listening skills are often a cause of a poor memory and it's easy to get into the habit of relying on a replay of what we've heard. Teachers often inadvertently encourage this by repeating instructions several times. In real life this isn't always possible, so it's useful for your pupils to learn to hear things properly on the first attempt.

Now reflect!

Questions to consider could include:

- Do you think you are a good listener? If not, how could you improve your listening?
- Why do you think a good thinker needs to be a good listener?
- Are there times when it's particularly important to listen really carefully?

Keep thinking

- Encourage your class to invent their own listening games in the playground or at home.
- Ask your pupils to consider some 'What if …' questions linked to the listening theme, e.g. What would it be like if …

    … we didn't have voices? … we all had identical voices? … animals made no sounds?

Follow-up ideas

Curriculum-based lesson

Repeat 'Mystery Voices' or create alternative listening games, e.g. ask pupils to select an object from the class and make a noise with it when chosen, while someone at the front tries to guess what the object was.

'All Ears!' fits best within subjects where precise drawing or colouring is needed, for example:

- Science – make a list of instructions for how to draw and label a simple diagram of the parts of a flower or the body.
- Mathematics – consolidate understanding of new spatial concepts by preparing instructions that use particular terms, e.g. straight and curved lines, words such as 'horizontal' and 'vertical', simple shapes and sets of objects.
- Supply outline pictures of buildings, people or scenes within History, Geography or Religious Studies, and give instructions for how to colour and label these.

Suggestions for display

Make a 'Good Listener Chart', to record pupils' names and examples of when they've followed instructions closely without needing to be told twice.

Notes for use by other year groups

Try using 'Mystery Voices' with foreign languages with older pupils. Present 'All Ears!' as a competition for groups or individuals and create more complex instructions, progressing to giving two or three of these at a time. Relate, for example, to:

- Drawing more difficult scientific diagrams or carrying out practical procedures.
- Producing more complicated mathematical tasks (either requiring pupils to draw something or to begin with a particular number and carry out a series of mathematical calculations).
- Labelling geographical maps.

Consider having a 'listening week' each half term when your pupils draw a face on their work at the end of each lesson – with a smile (if they feel they listened well), a straight mouth (if they feel their listening was average) or a frown (if their listening slipped).

Further resources

Mystery Voices is adapted from Robert Fisher's very useful book *Games for Thinking* (1997), Nash Pollock Publishing.

List of Year 1 resources provided on the CD Rom

Lesson 1   Metacognition
   Activity sheet: **My Magical Thinking Potion**
   Teacher instructions: **The Good Thinker Game**
   Activity cards: **The Good Thinker Game Cards** (3 pages)

Lesson 2   Questioning
   Poster: **Star Questions**
   Activity sheet: **Star Questions about ...**
   Poster: **Questioning for Understanding**
   Activity sheet: **Questioning for Understanding picture sheet**
   Teacher instructions: **Questioning for Understanding sample dialogues**

Lesson 3   Information skills
   Activity cards: **Odd One Out cards** (5 pages)

Lesson 4   Critical thinking
   Teacher instructions: **What am I?**
   Activity cards: **What am I? cards** (2 pages)
   Activity sheet: **Patchwork Thinking** (curriculum follow-up)

Lesson 5   Creative thinking
   Teacher instructions: **Start with a Squiggle**
   Activity sheet: **Use it or lose it!** (for more able/older pupils)

Lesson 6   Decision making
   Activity sheet: **Target Board ... perfect pet**
   Activity cards: **Target Board picture cards** (7 pages)
   Activity sheet: **Target Board** (curriculum follow-up)

Lesson 7   Memory skills
   Teacher instructions: **All Ears!**
   Activity sheet: **All Ears!**

'At a Glance' sample of Year 1 resources

These two pages shows a sample selection of activity sheets for this year group. These activities and many more can be found on the CD Rom.

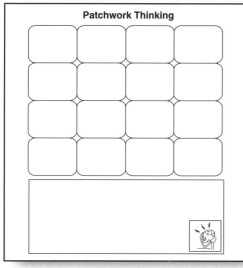

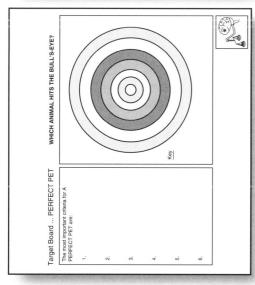

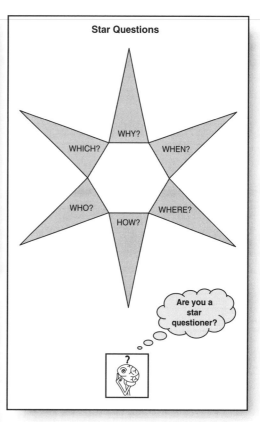

The Good Thinker Game cards 1

Have lots of ideas!	Be brave!
Stick with it!	Use your imagination!
Try to concentrate!	Listen carefully!
Ask for help!	Enjoy learning!
Learn from mistakes!	Ask questions!

Questioning for Understanding
Picture Sheet

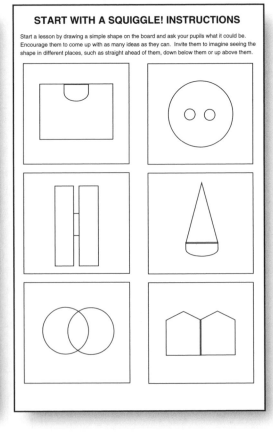

Odd One Out cards 1

SET ONE: FRUIT

SET TWO: HOMES

START WITH A SQUIGGLE! INSTRUCTIONS

Start a lesson by drawing a simple shape on the board and ask your pupils what it could be. Encourage them to come up with as many ideas as they can. Invite them to imagine seeing the shape in different places, such as straight ahead of them, down below them or up above them.

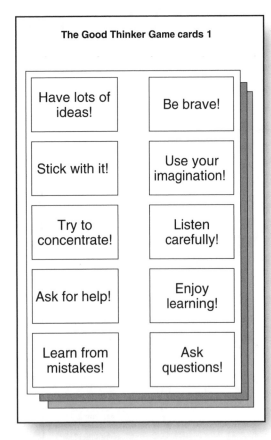

Lesson plans and resources

Lesson 1   **Metacognition**
First to Find …
Thinking about learning

Lesson 2   **Questioning**
Three 'Whys' Men
What do you wonder?

Lesson 3   **Information Skills**
Six Steps to Success
Flow diagrams

Lesson 4   **Critical thinking**
Tied Up in Knots!
Categories of Comparison

Lesson 5   **Creative thinking**
Connect!
Concept Collages

Lesson 6   **Decision Making**
Imagine that …
Weighing Up the Options

Lesson 7   **Memory Skills**
Spot the Difference
Memory Pictures

List of resources provided on the CD Rom

'At a Glance' sample of resources

Resources

Teacher instructions: **First to Find ...** 🔘
Activity sheet: individual copies of **First to Find ...** 🔘
Activity sheet: enlarged copy of **How can you recognise a good learner?** 🔘
Activity cards: a set of the **Good Learner cards** 🔘
Good Learner Certificates 🔘

Tune in!	C D	Activity: First to Find ...

- Play 'First to Find ..., following the instructions provided.
- Announce the winners and ask whose name appeared in each of the sections. If anyone wasn't mentioned, show where their name could have been used. Focus on the last box and share examples from the class of new things that have been learnt today.
- Explain that this game showed everyone has special talents and abilities: some are good at music, others at mathematics and others at getting along with people. The lists that the pupils made won't always be the same as we're learning new skills all the time. What's important is not so much the skills that we have now, but whether or not we can be good learners.

Heads together	

'Heads together' Introductory session   Page 146

Investigate	D G2	Thinking and Learning Tool: Thinking about learning

- If your pupils followed the programme in Year 1, ask them to remind you of the ingredients in their 'Good Thinking Potion'. Point out that, as they are getting older and more responsible, they are now ready to become more independent with their learning.
- Who thinks they are a good learner? Is this different from being a good thinker? How can you recognise a good learner when you meet one? What are their characteristics? Allow time to talk in pairs, then note ideas on the board. Use the sheet 'How can you recognise a good learner?' if working with a smaller group.
- Pick out particularly helpful ideas that illustrate important features of a good learner or suggest something that could be challenged.
- Assign a 'Good Learner card' to each pair and ask them to design a poster to help the class put it into practice. Encourage them to think of further examples to illustrate their point. (Any extra ideas raised by your class/can be included on blank cards.)
- Finish by asking each group to explain their poster to the class.

Helpful ! Hints

Your pupils' ideas about what makes a good learner are bound to overlap with Year 1's discussion about good thinkers, as the concepts are closely interrelated. For the purpose of this programme, learning skills focus on those habits and methods that help us become more effective in the way we *gather and absorb information*, while thinking skills focus on the processes we use to *transform this knowledge and generate new ideas*. If your pupils suggest that good learners are quiet, clever and get all the answers right, point out that this isn't necessarily the case. To engage in genuine learning will hurt! It's liberating for pupils to be told that the experience of 'being stuck' doesn't signal failure, but indicates their brains are being 'stretched'. What's important is how they deal with this. Use this lesson to reinforce those genuinely important thinking and learning dispositions (see page 23) that *everyone* can develop and to establish learning routines that will, with practice, become habits during the year.

Now reflect!

Questions to consider could include:

- What have we learnt about good learners?
- Who here thinks they are a good learner? In what way are you a good learner?
- How could you be a better learner? What are you going to try to do?

Keep thinking

Ask your pupils to make their own 'First to Find ...' grid sheets to show the characteristics of a good learner. Combine ideas to make a class version of the game.

Follow-up ideas

Unlike the following six lessons, there is no curriculum follow-up for the Metacognition lesson. However, you may still like to try the following:

- Talk to your class about your own ongoing experiences of learning and use these to model the positive learning behaviours that are being introduced. For example, tell them about a time when you found it hard learning something new, when you had to work together with someone else to discover how to do something or when you had to try lots of different sources to find the answers you needed.
- Get your pupils to make up a short item for a news programme about what it means to be a good learner. They could pretend to be reporters visiting a school and filming scenes from lessons or interviews with pupils and teachers. They might contrast this with clips from a school where the pupils have not learnt how to be good learners.
- Use the Good Learner Certificates to highlight positive learning behaviours.

Suggestions for display

Display the class posters as a reminder of the 'good learner characteristics' introduced.

Develop a wall display to assess and reward the pupils' journey towards becoming good learners. Display a photograph of each child at the beginning of a 'yellow-brick road', with eight clear stepping-stones leading to the 'Good Learner City'. Whenever a child receives a 'Good Learner Certificate' for a new characteristic, they move one step along the pathway.

Further resources

 Guy Claxton emphasises the importance of giving pupils the power to 'know what to do when you don't know what to do' and proposes many useful approaches to help with this. One is that classes spend time making posters containing suggestions for what to do in these 'stuck' situations, e.g. when you can't read a word, when a maths problem seems too complicated or when a tricky friendship problem has arisen.

For further reading, see *Building 101 Ways to Learning Power* by Maryl Chambers, Graham Powell and Guy Claxton (2004), Bristol: TLO Limited.

Year 2 | Lesson 2

Resources

Teacher instructions: **Three 'Whys' Men**
Activity sheet: individual copies of **What do you wonder?**
Activity sheet: **What do you *really* want to know?** (for more able/older pupils)

| **T**une in! | D C | Activity: Three 'Whys' Men |

- Write **YYY Men** on the board. Explain this is a word puzzle which requires your pupils to think in a different way. What you have written represents a phrase that they might be able to guess. What can they see on the board?
- Respond positively to all answers, prompting with alternative ways of asking the question if needed, e.g. 'How could you *say* what I have written on the board?' and 'Is that something that you hear people say?' A final hint is to cover up the 'Men' part and ask them to describe what they see now. Guide the discussion until they reach the answer 'Three Wise (Ys) Men'.
- Explain that good thinkers don't just accept what they are told, they ask questions and make sure they really understand what's going on. This game involves asking three 'Whys', which is a good way to check our understanding. Follow the instructions provided.

| **H**eads together | |

This lesson: Philosophy for Children, 'Generating the Question Session' Page 150
Curriculum lesson: Philosophy for Children, 'Discussion Session' Page 151
Discussion skill: Giving reasons for opinions. Encourage your class to support their statements with clear reasons or examples, using 'because ...'

| **I**nvestigate | D I G2/4 | Thinking and Learning Tool: What do you wonder? |

- Tell your pupils that good thinkers are curious about the world and enjoy asking 'What do I wonder?' This was how great thinkers in the past made new discoveries – by asking 'I wonder how that works?', 'I wonder why that happens?' or 'I wonder what would happen if ...?' They wondered what shape the world was, whether the Earth was stationary or moving, why things always fell down instead of up, what lay across the sea ... This type of question has no limits: we can wonder about whatever we want. Even if we can't always find the answers, it still helps us recognise how extraordinary the world around us is.
- Ask 2 or 3 volunteers to complete the sentence: 'I wonder why ...' and encourage them to use their imaginations and 'think big'.
- Repeat with the sentence starters 'I wonder if ...', then 'I wonder how ...'
- Use a 'think – pair – share' routine so pupils (a) spend some time individually, thinking of examples of 'I wonder' questions; (b) pair up and look at each other's ideas to see if this prompts more thoughts; then (c) work in groups to think of their best questions.
- Pupils then complete the 'What do you wonder?' sheet to record their favourite questions, illustrating these if they wish.

- A creative extension activity is to photocopy a selection of the pupils' 'I wonder' think bubbles for each group, then challenge them to find different ways of sorting them. When they have done this once and explained their reasoning, get them to try it again using a different method. Organise this activity as a competition and keep a record of how many different methods each group comes up with.

Model this process by giving examples of things that you wonder about, so your pupils see that questioning and learning are lifelong activities, rather than tasks restricted solely to school.

Now reflect!

Questions to consider could include:

- Which was your favourite of all the 'I wonder' questions?
- Why and when might it be useful to ask 'I wonder' questions?
- Do you think you have an enquiring nature? What could you do to develop this even more?

Keep thinking

Ask your pupils to talk to friends and family about what they wonder about and record the ideas that most interest them in an 'I wonder' journal. Share interesting thoughts at the end of each week.

Follow-up ideas

Curriculum-based lesson

Asking 'Why?' repeatedly is a good way to probe more deeply into pupils' understanding of curriculum subjects.

The 'I wonder' activity is also easy to apply to any curriculum area and helps to give pupils ownership of their own learning. At the beginning of a topic, ask your pupils what they wonder about that new subject. As before, encourage them to open their minds, to use their imagination and to 'think big'. Using the 'think – pair – share' routine can also be very helpful. In this way, for instance, a History, Religious Studies or Mathematics topic would begin with the pupils generating as many 'I wonder' questions as they can, then sorting these into different areas to investigate. You might then wish to structure your topic so that you cover each of these in turn.

Suggestions for display

✂ Cut out the 'I wonder' clouds and create a trail around the school – a 'Wonder Walk'. ✎ Blank clouds can be provided so other pupils can add their own ideas.

Notes for use by other year groups

The 'I wonder' activity provokes very interesting results with older pupils, who invariably raise all sorts of questions that they think about but don't usually have the chance to express. An interesting extension activity is to follow this up by challenging them to turn their ideas into an 'I wonder' poem. Within the curriculum, the sheet 'What do you really want to know?' can also be used.

Further resources

The 'Wonder Walk' activity was adapted from an idea in Guy Claxton's book *Building Learning Power* (2002) published by TLO Limited, Bristol, which suggested creating a 'Wonder Wall' to display questions.

A great source of more visual puns of the type used in the 'Tune in' activity is: http://www.norfacad.pvt.k12.va.us/puzzles/wacky.htm.

Resources

Activity sheet: enlarged group copies of **Six Steps to Success**

Activity cards: group sets of the **Six Steps to Success challenge cards**

Activity sheet: enlarged group copies of **Thinking with flow diagrams**

Activity cards: enlarged group sets of the **Flow diagram pictures**

Tune in!   G3 D   Activity: Six Steps to Success

- Invite your pupils to imagine they are teams of super-thinkers who are frequently asked to solve tricky problems. The secret of their success is that, whatever task they are given, they always think together as a team before drawing up a plan that shows the 6 steps they will take. They record the steps on the stepping stones of the sheet 'Six Steps to Success'.
- Ask each team to pick a challenge card and allow them a few minutes to think about and record their plan, either in words or pictures. Point out that, in real life, the first step would often be to get help from an adult – but for this exercise they need to think of other possibilities as well.
- Each group then reads out their card and presents their 6 steps. The other pupils should ask questions to clarify or challenge the plan.
- Talk about what the groups learnt from this game – what types of thinking have they used?

Heads together

This lesson:	Philosophy for Children, 'Generating the Question Session'	Page 150
Curriculum lesson:	Philosophy for Children, 'Discussion Session'	Page 151
Discussion skill:	Giving reasons for opinions. Encourage your class to support their statements with clear reasons or examples, using 'because ...'	

Investigate   D G3 I   Thinking and Learning Tool: Flow diagrams

- Tell your class you had 6 cartoon pictures that told a story, but accidentally they have become muddled up. Can they use the skills practised earlier to put the pictures in a logical order?
- Give each group a set of 'Flow diagram pictures' and the sheet 'Thinking with flow diagrams'. Allow 10 minutes for pupils to reach a decision and stick their pictures onto the sheet.
- Each group should then prepare and deliver a short presentation of their story, by describing each picture or acting out the events.
- After each presentation, invite the class to ask the group questions about their story to clarify particular points or to find out more about what happened.
- As an extension activity, ask your pupils to use another 'Thinking with flow diagrams' sheet to show what happened before the first picture or after the last.

Helpful Hints

Another version of this activity is to challenge the groups to find a second and then a third way of sequencing the pictures to create entirely different stories. In each case, emphasise the importance of collaborative group strategies such as listening, taking turns to offer ideas, giving clear reasons etc.

Now reflect!

Questions to consider could include:

- Can you think of other situations where it's important to make a careful plan with several clear steps?
- How well did your group work together? What were your strengths? How could you have improved?

Keep thinking

Ask your pupils to think of a problem that they have to solve this week and make a flow diagram to show the steps they will take.

Follow-up ideas

Curriculum-based lesson

Learning to sequence information in the most logical way is an important skill. Use the sheet 'Thinking with flow diagrams' within several curriculum or topic areas, such as:

- History – sequence a set of pictures or sentences describing key stages of a historical event, such as the Great Fire of London, then enact this in the form of a short play.
- Science – work out the logical order for cards containing the steps of a scientific experiment, represented in pictures or simple sentences. This helps pupils when they come to put the planned experiment into practice. Alternatively, sequence the stages of food's journey through the body or reinforce work on life cycles, by using pictures that represent the different stages of life of a plant, such as an oak tree, or an animal, such as a frog. Increase the challenge by leaving out one or two stages and asking your pupils to work out which steps are missing. As a creative follow-up activity, ask your pupils to invent their own animals and draw flow diagrams to show their stages of development.

Suggestions for display

✂ Create a large flow chart on the wall and, at the beginning of each week, put out 6 new pictures or sentences that can be moved around the chart until your pupils are happy with their decision. This could be an extension activity for more able pupils who finish work early.

Notes for use by other year groups

With older pupils, apply flow diagrams to more complex contexts, such as the water cycle or the formation of river features such as ox-bow lakes. Alternatively, use them to help structure ideas when planning a speech for a debate, a newspaper article or a story. More complicated versions of the flow diagram can be created by adding more steps or including a level of 'sub-steps' below.

For a great creative thinking activity to help children who find it hard to come up with story plots, cut out cartoons from magazines and newspapers and provide a different set of 6 pictures for each group. Allow 2 minutes to work together to form a 30-second story, which should then be told to the rest of the class. After hearing each group, shout 'Shuffle!' and ask them to move to a new table and sequence the pictures in a different way to make a completely new story. Again, listen to all the stories before moving to new tables.

Resources

Teacher instructions: **Tied Up in Knots!**
Activity sheet: enlarged group copies of **Categories of Comparison**
You will need to find: two types of fruit; two items or pictures for each group, e.g. chocolate bars or packets of crisps

Tune in!	G6	**Activity: Tied Up in Knots!**

- This is a great way of introducing logical thinking, but ideally requires quite a lot of space, so you may prefer to play it in a hall or in the playground.
- Follow instructions provided on the 'Tied Up in Knots!' sheet.
- Ask the pupils what sort of thinking they had to do for this game. What strategies did they use?

Heads together

This lesson:	Philosophy for Children, 'Generating the Question Session'	Page 150
Curriculum lesson:	Philosophy for Children, 'Discussion Session'	Page 151
Discussion skill:	Expressing agreement. Encourage your pupils to listen to each other and to respond when appropriate with 'I agree with … because …'	

Investigate	D G4	**Thinking and Learning Tool: Categories of Comparison**

- Hold up two different fruits. Ask your pupils what they would say if asked to 'compare and contrast these two items'.
- List ideas on the board in two unlabelled columns, representing differences and similarities. Encourage the pupils to suggest why there are two lists and to suggest suitable titles for them.
- Explain that, when asked to 'compare and contrast' two things, it's tempting to come up with lots of random ideas (as they did with the fruit), but that a good thinker would approach it more logically, listing the similarities first, then the differences. They might also group the ideas into 'categories of comparison', giving them names such as 'taste', 'smell', 'texture', 'pattern' and 'colour'. Relate this to the examples on the board.
- For the final stage, they must decide whether, overall, they think the two fruits are more different or more similar. How could this decision be made? Discuss ideas. Point out that, while counting ideas on each side is one possible method, it's also worth considering the *importance* of the differences and similarities. This may lead pupils to decide that, overall, the two items are more similar as they are both fruit, both healthy and both have skins, whereas their differences are just those of shape, colour and taste. Emphasise that there's no one right answer, so long as they give clear supporting reasons.
- Give each group the 'Categories of Comparison' sheet. The first 4 boxes are for similarities, the next 4 for differences and the grey boxes for category names. Allocate two items to each group and brainstorm several categories of comparison together.
- Allow time to carry out the activity. Finish by completing the sentence at the bottom of the sheet, using the structure: Overall, I think that —— and —— are more similar than different because … (or vice versa)
- Group conclusions, together with any interesting observations, should be shared.

This is a challenging task and your pupils are likely to need support. It's recommended that you use favourite food products such as types of chocolate bar or crisps, as this provides a motivating context! Categories of comparison could include shape, smell, wrapper design, ingredients, taste, colour and manufacturer.

Now reflect!

Questions to consider could include:

- You have done two very different activities in this lesson. Can you 'compare and contrast' them?
- Can you think of other times when you might have to 'untangle' something? Does this just apply to 'real' tangles? What's the best method to use to untangle our thinking?
- Are there other situations when it's necessary to compare and contrast two different things?

Keep thinking

Encourage your pupils to notice occasions when they are comparing two different options and to think about the criteria they use. A class record of these could be displayed.

Follow-up ideas

Curriculum-based lesson

The 'Categories of Comparison' activity provides a logical framework with which to approach 'compare and contrast' tasks. With younger pupils, subjects need to be kept quite simple, e.g. comparing:

- types of vehicle in a topic on transport
- animals in a topic on pets
- characters in a fairy tale
- plants or habitats, as part of a science topic

In each case, help pupils at the brainstorming stage when generating possible 'categories of comparison', until they become more familiar with this skill.

Suggestions for display

 Display a large 'Categories of Comparison' diagram, together with two different objects, photographs or pictures each week. Your pupils can suggest category names and, in spare moments or as a task for more able pupils, more specific points of comparison could be added.

Notes for use by other year groups

'Categories of Comparison' is a sophisticated analysis exercise, which in some ways is better suited to older pupils. However, this version of the standard 'compare and contrast' activity, if introduced early, provides a useful building block for later and teaches pupils to gather their ideas in a way that leads to much more rigorous and logical written work. It's worth spending time helping them learn how to structure the final summary, for example by offering useful phrases such as 'On balance ...', 'Weighing up the ideas on both sides ...' and 'While there are a greater number of similarities, the differences that exist are very important ...'.

With older pupils, introduce the method with food products or characters from favourite television programmes or cartoons. Within the curriculum, pupils could compare characters in books by the same author, historical figures, battles, geographical features or renewable energy sources, paintings or poems. Ideally follow with a consolidating task such as a letter to the local MP about an environmental decision or a transcript of an interview with two historical or fictitious characters (which could even be taped or recorded).

Resources

You will need to find: A3 paper, coloured board pens, magazines, coloured pencils.

Tune in!   C   Activity: Connect!

- Tell your pupils this game is designed to get them thinking quickly and creatively. Briefly discuss what 'thinking creatively' might mean and establish that it's about getting lots of new, original ideas.
- With your pupils standing in a circle, announce the starter word, e.g. rabbit. Take turns around the circle, each saying a word that's connected in some way to the previous word. After practising this once, increase the challenge by asking pupils to sit down if they (a) accidentally say a word that connects to an earlier word (often they will connect to the one before the previous one); (b) answer too slowly; or (c) repeat a word that has already been said.
- The winners are those left standing after two or three rounds of the circle.

Heads together

This lesson: Philosophy for Children, 'Generating the Question Session'   Page 150
Curriculum lesson: Philosophy for Children, 'Discussion Session'   Page 151
Discussion skill: Expressing agreement. Encourage your pupils to listen to each other and to respond when appropriate with 'I agree with ... because ...'

Investigate   D   G2   I   Thinking and Learning Tool: Concept Collages

- Tell your pupils that good creative thinkers (a) know how important it is to have lots of ideas before picking their best idea and (b) enjoy looking for new and interesting connections between these ideas.
- In the centre of the board, write the word 'Imagination'. As with the game earlier, ask for suggestions of words linked to this word. Note these on the board, in different colours and writing styles, drawing arrows in one colour out from your central word.
- Ask a volunteer to pick one of these words and repeat the process, using a new colour to draw arrows from this word out to its connected words.
- Give pupils 2 minutes to work in pairs to choose another word from the board and think of further connecting ideas, before sharing their best ideas with the class. These should be added to the Concept Collage that is forming, using different coloured arrows for each 'starter word'.
- Pupils can then work on their own Concept Collages of the word 'Imagination', using ideas from the board, their own thoughts and plenty of colours, symbols and pictures to cover as much of the page as possible. Possible themes include:

  - linked processes such as daydreaming, inventing, drawing and writing
  - names of imaginative things such as television programmes, stories, songs or poems, imaginative pictures cut out from magazines

The purpose of this activity is to encourage pupils to see creative thinking as a journey: each step leads to another step; each idea leads to another idea. The ideal approach is enthusiastic, uncritical and fun – you are looking for impractical, silly ideas as well as more sensible ones as this stage is about generation, not evaluation.

Now reflect!

Questions to consider could include:

- Which is the funniest/cleverest/most interesting linked idea on your Concept Collage?
- What other words would be interesting to explore using a Concept Collage?

Keep thinking

Ask your pupils to make a Concept Collage of a topic of their choice – for example, a hobby, a pet, their home, a holiday or a person they know.

Follow-up ideas

Curriculum-based lesson

Concept Collages provide a practical and visual means of exploring an idea or a topic. They work especially well in the middle of a topic, to keep up the momentum and interest by bringing in fresh ideas when the initial more obvious connections have already been made.

With younger pupils, they can be applied to a very wide range of areas:

- Cross-disciplinary topics – such as 'Games', 'Transport', 'Pets', 'Weather' or 'Holidays'.
- Science/History/Geography/Religious Studies – to brainstorm ideas related to topics such as forces, electricity, local environment or a particular place of worship.
- English/History – to explore the life and personalities of characters from books or people from the past, such as 'Horrid Henry' (Henry VIII) or Florence Nightingale
- PSHE – to think about more abstract concepts such as 'family' and 'friendship'.

Suggestions for display

Display the Concept Collages under a title such as 'What is imagination?' and include reminders such as 'Creative thinkers don't worry about how their ideas sound', 'Creative thinkers have lots of ideas before choosing their best one' and 'Creative thinkers find interesting links between ideas'.

Notes for use by other year groups

With older pupils, the 'Connect' game is a very popular warm-up activity and can be played along-side 'Disconnect!', which is described in Year 5, Lesson 4.

Concept Collages can be used to:

- Unpick abstract concepts such as emotions (anger, love, courage), characteristics (beauty, humility, curiosity), subjects (history, art) or those linked with current affairs (democracy, war).
- Encourage a deeper study of curriculum topics, such as Mathematics (investigating connections within a topic such as fractions or shapes) or Geography (examining the meaning of 'culture' and exploring the culture of a particular country).

Resources

Activity sheet: enlarged group copies of **Weighing Up the Options** 💿
You will need to find: a set of pan-balance scales, sticky labels, a selection of plastic building bricks of identical shape and size

Tune in!	C	Activity: Imagine that …

- With your pupils in a circle, invite them to imagine that they have been asked to design a completely new type of shoe that everyone would want to own. What could make it special?
- Take turns to offer suggestions. If a child chooses to 'pass', return to him or her later.
- Praise everyone for their ideas and remind them this is always the first stage of any creative thinking task.
- Which idea might be the most successful in reality? What's good about the idea? Are there any problems with it?

Heads together

This lesson: Philosophy for Children, 'Generating the Question Session'   Page 150
Curriculum lesson: Philosophy for Children, 'Discussion Session'   Page 151
Discussion skill: Expressing disagreement. Encourage your pupils to listen to each other and to respond when appropriate with 'I disagree with … because …'

Investigate	D G4	Thinking and Learning Tool: Weighing Up the Options

- When do we make decisions? How many examples of decisions have your pupils made today? (Point out that the 'Imagine that … activity involved making a decision.) Do we always make good decisions? Can you remember any bad decisions you have made?
- Explain that, when making an important decision – just as with creative thinking – the first step is to come up with lots of possible ideas, then the next is to pick the best option.
- Ask your pupils to imagine they could be in charge of the school for a day and could introduce one new rule. Brainstorm options and list these on the board.
- How could they decide which is the best idea? Reveal the pan-balance scales and introduce the idea that decision making is rather like weighing: when considering an option, you can put its good points on one side and its bad points on the other.
- Select one option for focus and ask the class to suggest its good points. Write each idea on a sticky label, attach it to a plastic brick and place it in one side of the scales. Repeat for the bad points.
- Which side is heavier? The scales show whether – 'on balance' – the option was a good or a bad idea.
- Give each group a 'Weighing Up the Options' sheet and introduce a new decision: if they could be any animal for one day, what would they choose? Allow time for groups to work through the sheet, supporting them where necessary.
- Finish with groups presenting their final decision and reasoning.

Model the process of decision making by sharing a story that tells your class about a decision you have had to make recently. You could even ask your pupils to help you consider the good and bad points.

Now reflect!

Questions to consider could include:

- What was good about working as a group? What was difficult?
- Why is it important to make decisions carefully?
- Can you think of any situations where you could use this method?

Keep thinking

Encourage your pupils to notice the 'decision moments' they encounter during the week and to use the 'Weighing Up the Options' method to consider the good and bad points of the different options.

Follow-up ideas

Curriculum-based lesson

Select a suitable decision that can be discussed within the context of a curriculum subject without becoming too complicated. The key to choosing an appropriate decision is to check whether it makes sense to generate lots of options, then to consider one in more depth by weighing up the arguments for and against that option, for example:

- English – use a decision faced by a character in a book to work out what they should do next, e.g. When Little Red Riding Hood realised the wolf was dressed as her grandmother, what should she have done?
- History – if I lived the past, which famous character would I like to have been?
- Geography – which would be the most suitable location for a settlement?

Suggestions for display

 Display a decision next to the scales each week, e.g. 'If I could be a famous sportsperson, I think I might choose to be a footballer' or 'If I could have any pet I wanted, I think I might choose a penguin'. In spare moments, pupils can note plus and minus points on sticky labels, attach them to the plastic bricks and add them to the scales. At the end of the week, your class can guess which side is heavier, before checking by reading out the 'plus' and 'minus' bricks.

Notes for use by other year groups

With older pupils, refer to the two sides as 'arguments for' and 'arguments against'. After the initial brainstorming of ideas, each group could pick one of the options to investigate and research, before presenting it to the class. Examples could include:

- History – what was the main cause of the Second World War? What was the most important invention/new law of the Victorians?
- Science – if you could visit any planet, which would you choose?
- PSHE – what is the most dangerous consequence of smoking?
- Geography – which type of natural disaster has had the most impact on the world?

Further resources

 Further examples of 'Imagine that …' activities and creative decision making situations can be found in 'Just Suppose …' and 'Just Suppose … Too' by C.J. Simister, published by learn4life, www.learn4life.co.uk.

Resources

Teacher instructions: **Memory Pictures**
Activity sheet: enlarged copy of **Memory Pictures**, ideally mounted onto board
You will need to find: A3 paper for each group

Tune In! **D** **Activity: Spot the Difference**

- Choose 3 pupils to stand at the front and allow your class one minute to look closely at them.
- The pupils leave the room and each alter one aspect of their appearance, e.g. two could swap shoes, one remove a hair grip, pull socks down etc.
- On their return, the others should try to identify the differences.
- Repeat several times.
- Ask pupils why they played this game. Explain that this lesson's focus is improving the memory and that developing good skills of observation is a good place to start. Often what we think we have forgotten is something we failed to notice properly in the first place.

Heads together

This lesson: Philosophy for Children, 'Generating the Question Session'   Page 150
Curriculum lesson: Philosophy for Children, 'Discussion Session'   Page 151
Discussion skill: Expressing disagreement. Encourage your pupils to listen to each other and to respond when appropriate with 'I disagree with ... because ...'

Investigate **D** **G4** **Thinking and Learning Tool: Diamond Ranking**

- Have the enlarged and mounted sheet 'Memory Pictures' at the front of the class, with the diagram hidden.
- Seat each group around a table with plenty of space. Explain that the pupils are going to take part in a team memory challenge which will require them to use the skills of observation they developed earlier.
- Follow the instructions provided on the sheet 'Memory Pictures'.
- Afterwards, ask the groups to turn their pictures face down.
- Ask questions about the diagram, such as:

  - What type of things had labels on the diagram? (e.g. equipment, rooms, furniture)
  - Which rooms/pieces of equipment can you remember? Where were they on the diagram?
  - How did you remember where they went?
  - How many beds were in each dormitory?
  - Name the room at the north side of the sports hall etc.

- Look at the diagrams and announce the winning group.

Helpful Hints

Memory Pictures is a lively, entertaining game that your pupils will enjoy. Keep the pace fast and monitor behaviour to ensure no one is left out or ignored. If problems arise, pause the activity and encourage groups to reflect and consider whether they are making the best use of each of their members' knowledge of the picture.

Now reflect!

Questions to consider could include:

- What strategies did you use? (e.g. dividing the picture into parts, taking one section at a time)
- Do you feel you worked successfully as a group? What methods might you use next time?
- Did this method help you to remember the diagram?

Keep thinking

Encourage your pupils to be 'Thinking Detectives' (a theme that's raised later in the programme) and, each day, to try to spot something around the school that they have never noticed before.

Follow-up ideas

Curriculum-based lesson

'Memory Pictures' improves memory skills and reinforces understanding of the focus diagram. It can be used in several subjects, e.g.

- Science – a diagram showing the parts of a plant or body; or a particular electrical circuit.
- Geography – a map of the local neighbourhood, town or country. Depending on the focus of your topic, you might ask pupils to remember and place names of towns and cities, rivers, mountains or other features. Alternatively, use a plan of the school with some spaces left empty, so the pupils can follow this up by walking around the school to fill in the missing labels.
- Religious Studies – a plan of a religious building, such as a mosque or a church.

A useful way of preparing pupils for a school outing is to use this activity with a plan of the site (e.g. museum, study centre etc.) that they are going to visit.

In each case, choose whether it's realistic to expect the groups to reproduce the whole diagram or whether it's more appropriate to give them some form of outline, e.g. with the shape of the United Kingdom or the human body already printed onto it.

Suggestions for display

Keep a chart on display to record the class's 'Keep thinking' observations. Illustrate with a picture of a detective with a magnifying glass and the title, 'This week, we have noticed …'

Notes for use by other year groups

This activity is popular with all ages and is an excellent revision exercise as pupils tend to remember details much more clearly afterwards. With older pupils, increase the level of detail and sophistication of the diagram, for example:

- Geography – use a more complex map, a diagram of the water cycle or a cross-section of a volcano.
- History – use a particular monarch's family tree or a diagram of a typical medieval or Tudor house or village.
- Mathematics – reproduce an abstract picture containing shapes, angles and lines, involving specific vocabulary and precision measuring as well as observation and memory.

Further resources

'Spot the Difference' can be found in Robert Fisher's very useful book *Games for Thinking* (1997), published by Nash Pollock Publishing.

List of Year 2 resources provided on the CD Rom

Lesson 1   Metacognition
     Teacher instructions: **First to find …**
     Activity sheet: **First to find …**
     Activity sheet: **How can you recognise a good learner?**
     Activity cards: **Good Learner cards** (2 pages)

Lesson 2   Questioning
     Teacher instructions: **Three 'Whys' Men**
     Activity sheet: **What do you wonder?**
     Activity sheet: **What do you *really* want to know?** (for more able/older pupils)

Lesson 3   Information skills
     Activity sheet: **Six Steps to Success**
     Activity cards: **Six Steps to Success challenge cards**
     Activity sheet: **Thinking with flow diagrams**
     Activity cards: **Flow diagram pictures**

Lesson 4   Critical thinking
     Teacher instructions: **Tied Up in Knots!**
     Activity sheet: **Categories of Comparison**

Lesson 5   Creative thinking
     No resources required

Lesson 6   Decision making
     Activity sheet: **Weighing Up the Options**

Lesson 7   Memory skills
     Teacher instructions: **Memory Pictures**
     Activity sheet: **Memory Pictures**

'At a Glance' sample of Year 2 resources

These two pages show a sample selection of activity sheets for this year group. These activities and many more can be found on the CD Rom.

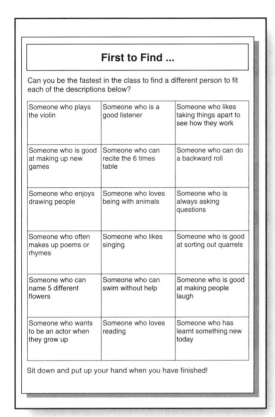

First to Find ...

Can you be the fastest in the class to find a different person to fit each of the descriptions below?

Someone who plays the violin	Someone who is a good listener	Someone who likes taking things apart to see how they work
Someone who is good at making up new games	Someone who can recite the 6 times table	Someone who can do a backward roll
Someone who enjoys drawing people	Someone who loves being with animals	Someone who is always asking questions
Someone who often makes up poems or rhymes	Someone who likes singing	Someone who is good at sorting out quarrels
Someone who can name 5 different flowers	Someone who can swim without help	Someone who is good at making people laugh
Someone who wants to be an actor when they grow up	Someone who loves reading	Someone who has learnt something new today

Sit down and put up your hand when you have finished!

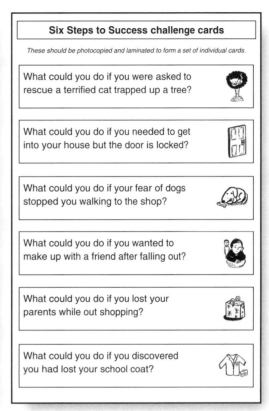

Six Steps to Success challenge cards

These should be photocopied and laminated to form a set of individual cards.

What could you do if you were asked to rescue a terrified cat trapped up a tree?

What could you do if you needed to get into your house but the door is locked?

What could you do if your fear of dogs stopped you walking to the shop?

What could you do if you wanted to make up with a friend after falling out?

What could you do if you lost your parents while out shopping?

What could you do if you discovered you had lost your school coat?

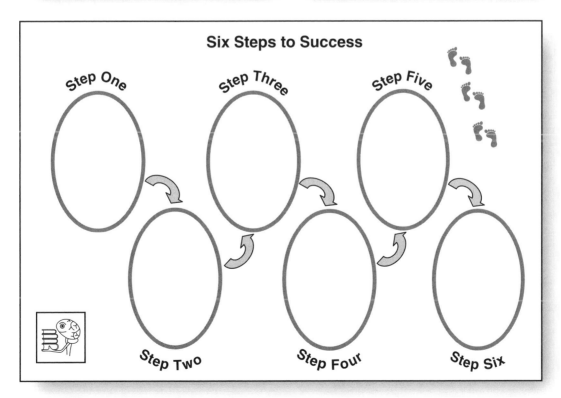

Six Steps to Success

Step One

Step Three

Step Five

Step Two

Step Four

Step Six

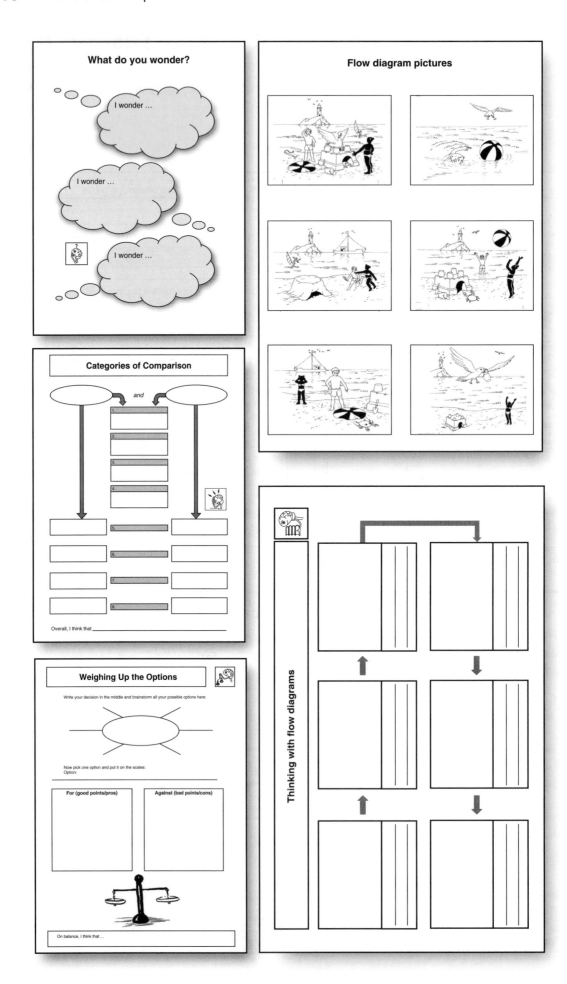

Year 3

Lesson plans and resources

Resources

Activity sheet: individual copies of **A Recipe for Good Thinking and Learning** 💿
Teacher checklist: 20 Dispositions of an Active Thinker and Learner 💿

Tune in　　　C　　　Activity: I'm Good at …

- Ask your pupils to choose one of their strengths, e.g. writing poems, playing football, making friends. With everyone standing in a circle, pick a starter person to complete the sentence 'I'm good at … ' and add an action to represent this.
- The next person repeats the first sentence and action, then adds one of their own. For example, if the first child said 'I'm good at telling jokes' and mimed someone bent double with laughter, the second child might say, 'X is good at telling jokes' (same mime as before) 'and I'm good at drawing cats' (adding a new mime for this idea). Each person should try to remember all previous contributions.
- The game continues until everyone's had a turn. Encourage your pupils to help each other with prompts.
- Finish by pointing out how many different talents there are in the class.

Heads together

'Heads together' Introductory session　　　　　　　　　　　　　　　　　　　Page 146

Investigate　　D　I　G2　　Thinking and Learning Tool: A Recipe for Good Thinking and Learning

- Point out that people often know their practical strengths, e.g. art, mathematics or sport. However, because we concentrate more on talking about '*what* to think and *what* to learn' rather than '*how* to think and *how* to learn', we often don't know how to decide whether we are *good at* thinking and learning. The good news is that everyone can learn to be a better thinker and a better learner: they just need the right ingredients.
- Explain that the class is going to create a special recipe for good thinking and learning. Gather examples of 'recipe language' (e.g. 'Add a pinch of …', 'Stir in two spoonfuls of …') and note these at the side of the board.
- Discuss your pupils' ideas about ingredients. While the aim is to allow them to direct the discussion as much as possible, try to link their ideas with the points on the sheet '20 Dispositions of an Active Thinker and Learner'. Also mention other more practical 'ingredients', such as 'plenty of sleep', 'frequent short breaks' and 'a healthy diet'.
- Use a 'think – pair – share' approach: after the first 2 or 3 suggestions, allow some silent thinking time (when they can look out of the window, put their heads on their desk etc.), then some time to discuss thoughts with a partner and generate more ideas. Finally, ask each pair to contribute their top thinking and learning ingredient for the recipe.
- When lots of ideas are listed on the board, ask your pupils to complete the sheet 'A Recipe for Good Thinking and Learning' by selecting those ingredients they feel are most valuable.
- Finish by asking volunteers to read their recipes.

Explain that, by putting the recipe into practice, we are developing our 'thinking and learning muscles'. Remind your pupils that real thinking and learning 'hurts' (a concept introduced in Year 2), as it's exercising the mind – just as our bodies hurt when pushed to their physical limits. This experience should be viewed positively as a sign that genuine learning is taking place. Teach them to recognise the natural 'pain and panic' response, take a deep breath, stop and think and then try again, perhaps by looking at things in a different way, trying a new approach, checking their results and then asking for help if it's really needed.

Now reflect!

Questions to consider could include:

- What is the one most important ingredient in the thinking and learning recipe?
- Which ingredient do you have most of? Which do you have least of?
- What could you do to develop more of your weakest ingredient?

Keep thinking

Encourage your pupils to take their recipes home and to ask their parents and anyone else at home for ideas of other ingredients that may have missed out.

Follow-up ideas

Unlike the following six lessons, there is no curriculum follow-up for the Metacognition lesson. However, you may still like to try some of the following:

- Encourage your pupils to ask older members of their family to tell them about a difficult learning experience that they faced. How did they overcome it?
- Repeat the 'Tune In!' game using the sentence, 'I'm a good thinker/learner because ...' and adding actions to represent the ideas.
- Ask your class to find out about real people whose lives demonstrated the ingredients from the thinking and learning recipe. Tell them about Thomas Edison, inventor of the electric light bulb, who, when a friend tried to console him about his failed experiments, said 'Why, I have not failed. I've just found 10,000 ways that won't work' (Dryden G. and Vos J. (2001) *The Learning Revolution.* Visions of Education, p. 281).

Suggestions for display

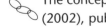 Take photographs of each of your pupils adopting a 'thinking pose' of their own choice and write their chosen ingredient in a think bubble next to them.

Further resources

The concept of 'thinking and learning muscles' is introduced by Guy Claxton in *Building Learning Power* (2002), published by TLO Limited, Bristol.

Resources

Poster: **Remember to ask Thinking Questions**
Activity sheet: individual copies of **My Thinking Questions**
You will need to find: a simple object, e.g. an apple

Tune in	C		Activity: Twenty Questions

- Challenge your class to discover what object you are thinking of. They can ask up to 20 questions, to which you will only reply 'yes' or 'no'.
- If the object hasn't been guessed after 10 attempts, ask your pupils to consider their methods. They should realise that simply guessing uses too many questions and that more careful strategies are needed. Ask for examples of general questions that would help narrow down the options.
- Continue the game and repeat with volunteers choosing starter objects and answering the questions. Afterwards, ask your class to decide on their top 5 tips for winning the game.

Heads together

This lesson: Philosophy for Children, 'Generating the Question Session'   Page 150
Curriculum lesson: Philosophy for Children, 'Discussion Session'   Page 151
Discussion skill: Expressing agreement and disagreement. Encourage your class to respond with 'I agree with ... because ...' and 'I disagree with ... because ...'

Investigate	D	G4	Thinking and Learning Tool: Asking 'Thinking Questions'

- Ask your class to recall ingredients of their recipe from Lesson 1. Remind them that good thinkers enjoy asking questions as these help them discover more about the world around them.
- Are all questions interesting? Can anyone think of any really boring questions? Distinguish between two types of questions: 'Right Answer Questions' (closed questions with just one possible right answer) and 'Thinking Questions'. What might a 'Thinking Question' be? Gather ideas, such as:
  - It has lots of possible answers
  - It makes us think really hard
  - It leads to an interesting discussion where we share ideas
- Explain that coming up with 'Thinking Questions' can be difficult initially, so it helps to have some 'thinking question stems'. Read and display the poster 'Remember to ask Thinking Questions'.
- Hold up an object, such as an apple. Your pupils should alternate between asking one 'Right Answer Question' and one 'Thinking Question', using the poster to help them.
- Repeat the activity with your pupils standing in a circle and a volunteer in the centre as the focus for questions. Sample questions include:
  - Right Answer Questions: How old is X? Where does X live? Does X have a pet?
  - Thinking Questions: How do we know that X is happy? What might X be when he/she grows up? How could we find out what X's favourite hobby is?
- Your pupils should use the sheet 'My Thinking Questions' to record 8 interesting and imaginative questions about anything at all, each beginning with a different stem.
- At the end, ask them to put a star next to their favourite question and share these.

The circle activity is popular and fun if done carefully. Pupils should ask positive questions only and the volunteer can 'pass' rather than answer a question whenever they want.

Now reflect!

Questions to consider could include:

- Why is it important to ask 'Thinking Questions'?
- Do you think you ask more 'Right Answer Questions' or more 'Thinking Questions'?
- Can you come up with a questioning motto for the class, to encourage everyone to be curious about things around them?

Keep thinking

Follow up this lesson with a research-based activity to encourage your pupils to investigate one of their chosen questions.

Follow-up ideas

Curriculum-based lesson

There are two ways of developing this method in the curriculum:

(1)   To introduce a topic or section

At the beginning of a new topic, give an enlarged copy of 'My Thinking Questions' to each group and allow them time to select their top 8 questions. Each group should then type their questions into a single class document that can be copied for everyone. Their next task is to find a logical way of organising these into subsets. The topic can then become an investigation into each of these areas, encouraging your pupils to see learning as something they are driving themselves. (Not that topics chosen will frequently be the ones you hope to cover!)

(2)   Using a source of your choice
Use the sheet to focus on something specific, e.g.:

- History – a historical artefact, photograph, picture, diary entry or eye witness account.
- English – a newspaper article, chapter or page from a book, poem or play.
- Art – a painting by an artist that the class is studying.
- Religious Studies – a picture of a place of worship, a religious article, story or parable.
- Science – a diagram, experiment or piece of equipment.

Pupils could work in groups, in pairs or individually. A combination can prove effective – with pupils working alone initially, then pairing up with a partner and sharing ideas, before finally working together as a group. Time should be found to share each child's favourite question.

Suggestions for display

✂ Display the class's chosen questions when beginning a topic or use the ones from this lesson. Whenever an answer is discovered, get your pupils to add it to the display.

Further resources

 A useful questioning website is: http://questioning.org/Q7/toolkit.html

Resources

Teacher instructions: **Tree Diagram Challenge**
Activity cards: group sets of **Tree Diagram Challenge words**
Activity sheet: enlarged group copies of **Tree Diagram Challenge**
Teacher instructions: **Make your own Mind Map® and Mandala**
Activity sheet: enlarged individual copies of **Make your own Mind Map® and Mandala**

Tune in!   G3   Activity: Tree Diagram Challenge

- Give each group an enlarged copy of the sheet 'Tree Diagram Challenge' and follow the instructions provided
- After the activity, ask your class what skills they were using. How did they work together as a group? What would their tips be for teams playing this game in the future?
- Ask them to consider other contexts where this might be a useful tool for displaying information.

Heads together

This lesson: Philosophy for Children, 'Generating the Question Session'   Page 150
Curriculum lesson: Philosophy for Children, 'Discussion Session'   Page 151
Discussion skill: Expressing agreement and disagreement. Encourage your class to respond with 'I agree with ...because ...' and 'I disagree with ... because ...'

Investigate   D   G4   Thinking and Learning Tool: Visual Mapping

- Give out the sheet 'Make your Own Mind Map® and Mandala' and explain these two methods are useful ways of organising information. As they make use of colours and pictures as well as words, some people find them more memorable than normal notes.
- Talk through the two methods one step at a time, using the instructions provided and allowing plenty of time for the pupils to build up their two diagrams gradually. The same topic is used for both to allow easy comparison.
- Judge how detailed the Mandalas and Mind Maps® should become for this first practice exercise. Your pupils will vary in how quickly they adapt to these methods, so it may be appropriate to allow some to make more detailed diagrams, while encouraging others to keep their diagrams quite simple.

Helpful
!
Hints

The 3 methods introduced here are useful tools and can play a significant role in helping children to gather, organise and analyse ideas and information. You may prefer to introduce them separately and more slowly over more than one lesson. However, if your class are able to learn the methods together, it can prove a very useful exercise in comparison.

Now reflect!

Questions to consider could include:F

- Which of the three visual mapping methods do you prefer at this stage? Why? What are the similarities between them? What are the differences?
- Can you think of situations when it would be useful to make a Tree Diagram, Mind Map® or Mandala?
- Could you turn the information on your sheet into a Tree Diagram? How? Would it be better in any way?

Keep thinking

Ask your pupils to make a Tree Diagram, Mind Map® or Mandala of a topic of their choice, e.g. their favourite hobby, a television programme or a holiday.

Follow-up ideas

Curriculum-based lesson

Find plenty of opportunities to practise these visual mapping methods as it takes time to become familiar with the techniques, to learn how to divide topics into sections and to discover which map is most suitable for different contexts. Try the following 4 methods to integrate them into the curriculum:

1. **Mapping as a summarising or revision aid** – pupils can look through their notes and make a Tree Diagram, Mind Map® or Mandala of them. This could be stuck on their wall to act as a quick visual reminder of the topic.
2. **Mapping as a challenge to consolidate understanding** – give out sets of important topic words to be sorted logically using one of these structures. The number of levels, branches, circles etc. can be altered to fit your theme and you can use font size or colour as a clue if necessary.
3. **Mapping as a planning tool** – when writing a story or beginning a project, pupils can use these diagrams to record their ideas and to plan a structure for their work.
4. **Mapping as an opening activity** – to show what pupils already know about a topic you are just beginning.

Suggestions for display

Get groups of pupils to work together to create their own displays that teach people how to make a Tree Diagram, a Mind Map® and a Mandala.

 ### Notes for use by other year groups

It is important that these skills are reinforced throughout the school, so that your pupils can choose which methods they find most helpful. Younger pupils can be introduced to all three visual maps in a simpler format, while older pupils can also try two more challenging activities:

- Groups can work together to make their own sets of words to use in a Tree Diagram, Mind Map® or Mandala. Afterwards, they could swap sets and try each others' challenges.
- Teams of pupils can be given a different article or piece of text each and challenged to devise visual maps to draw out the main areas, important points and interesting details. This is a challenging activity that really serves to consolidate understanding of the text. Afterwards these should form the basis for presentations to the class.

Further resources

 Mind Map® is a registered trademark of the Buzan Organisation Limited 1990. For more information, contact: BUZAN CENTRES WORLDWIDE PLC, www.Buzancentresworldwide.com.

Tony Buzan has written many books on the subject, including *Mind Mapping for Kids* (2003) London: Thorsons, which outlines the process and gives lots of practical examples in language that is easily accessible.

Mandala Thinking was devised at Northwood College based on an idea of A. Pearson.

Year 3 — Lesson 4

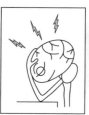

Resources

Teacher instructions: **Su Doku puzzles** (2 pages) 🌐
Activity sheet: individual copies of **Su Doku puzzles** 🌐
Activity sheet: enlarged group copies of **Define it!** 🌐
You will need to find: a dictionary

Tune in!   [D] [I]   Activity: Su Doku puzzles

- Su Dokus puzzles provide a useful introduction to logical thinking as they help to clarify the difference between what is possibly true and what is definitely true.
- Use the instruction sheet to work through the simple practice examples.
- Allow time for your pupils to attempt the 'Su Doku puzzles' sheet individually, to ensure all have equal access to the activity.
- Pause the lesson and clarify methods where needed. Encourage your pupils to check their answers very carefully.

Heads together

This lesson: Philosophy for Children, 'Generating the Question Session'   Page 150
Curriculum lesson: Philosophy for Children, 'Discussion Session'   Page 151
Discussion skill: Taking a 'thinking moment'. Encourage your class to stop and think for a moment before responding to the previous person's idea.

Investigate   [D] [G4]   Thinking and Learning Tool: Define it!

- Write the word 'pizza' in the middle of the board and draw a large circle around it.
- Ask your pupils to tell you some facts about pizzas, e.g. 'they have cheese on top', 'they are round' and 'they are tasty'. Note all ideas inside the circle.
- Tell them that good logical thinkers are interested in the difference between things that *have to be* true and things that just *might be* true or are *sometimes* true. Ask them which of the ideas in the circle are *always* true of pizzas? Answers might include 'They were invented in Italy' and 'They have a base of some sort of bread'. Draw lines in one colour from the central word radiating out to these descriptions.
- Next, ask which ideas are *usually* true of pizzas. Draw lines using a different colour out to these characteristics.
- Explain that your pupils have done something very clever here: they have worked out what a pizza *really* is by developing a definition of what the word 'pizza' means. From this diagram, it's a short step to completing the sentence, A pizza is something which … *(insert characteristics that are always true)*. It usually … *(insert characteristics that are usually true)* and may sometimes … *(insert any other characteristics that are sometimes true)*.
- Ask the class where they would find another definition of a pizza. Show them a dictionary and ask a volunteer to read out how it defines the word. What are the similarities and differences?
- Allocate each group a different word (e.g. friend, mobile phone, pet, party, game, hero) and get them to use enlarged copies of the sheet 'Define it!' to work out a logical definition.
- Afterwards, ask each group to read out their definition, then compare it with the dictionary definition.

Choose different words to investigate if you prefer, but try to select a concept that is universally recognised. If you can bring in some sample pizza packaging or pictures of pizzas of different types, this can prove useful when the children are generating ideas.

Now reflect!

Questions to consider could include:

- What sort of thinking did you use to work out your definitions?
- How would you know if someone was a good logical thinker? What would they do?
- When is it important to think carefully and logically?

Keep thinking

Set your pupils another 'Define it!' challenge. For instance, you could ask them to see if they can work out the key characteristics of a vehicle, a family or a teacher.

Follow-up ideas

Curriculum-based lesson

The 'Define it!' activity is challenging but useful, as it encourages children to break an object or topic into its component parts, then consider which of these parts are critical for its existence. This type of logical thinking activity can lead to a deeper understanding of the topic at hand. Some possible curriculum options include:

- Religious Studies – considering the key characteristics of a particular religious building ties in well with a visit to a mosque or church for example.
- English – discussing the key characteristics of a book or a writing genre, e.g. a nursery rhyme or a fairy tale.
- Science – identifying the key characteristics of a flowering plant, a circuit or a metal.

Suggestions for display

Display a word or picture and involve pupils in generating the lines and labels. Change this frequently.

✂ Notes for use by other year groups

Select more challenging concepts for older pupils to define, such as:

- Religious Studies – apply to a place of worship *in general*, requiring pupils to bring together various aspects of their knowledge about the different buildings they have studied.
- English – investigate further forms of writing, e.g. poems, letters, newspaper articles, metaphors, science fiction stories or plays. Provide several short excerpts of your chosen type of writing so your pupils can analyse these and draw out their common features. Alternatively, consider the key characteristics of a villain or a hero, by comparing several different stories.
- Art – supply several pieces of work by a particular artist and challenge your class to seek out the key characteristics of this artist's work.
- Geography – find the key characteristics of a map, a hurricane or a mountain.
- Science – discuss the key characteristics of a solid, a liquid or a gas.

Further resources

Use simple Su Doku Puzzles with children as early as Year 1 and 2. Printable Su Doku puzzles for a range of abilities can be found on: http://www.activityvillage.co.uk/sudoku_for_kids.htm.

Resources

Activity sheet: enlarged group copies of **Lateral Links**

Tune in!	**C**	**Activity: Tree Diagram Challenge**

- Explain that sometimes even good creative thinkers get a block when their mind goes blank and they can't think of an idea. However, instead of worrying about it, they look for a way around it. One such way is 'reverse thinking', which considers the *opposite* question to the one you need to solve.
- Get your pupils to stand in a circle and take turns to suggest ways to solve one (or more) of the following problems:

  o What is the best way to lose a football match?

  o What is the best way to be late for school?

  o What is the best way to be bored in the playground?

- Can they think of any other situations where this method could help stimulate thinking?

Heads together		

This lesson:	Philosophy for Children, 'Generating the Question Session'	Page 150
Curriculum lesson:	Philosophy for Children, 'Discussion Session'	Page 151
Discussion skill:	Taking a 'thinking moment'. Encourage your class to stop and think for a moment before responding to the previous person's idea.	

Investigate	**D** **G4**	**Thinking and Learning Tool: Lateral Links**

- Ask the class to call out 10 different nouns and write these on the board. Emphasise that they can be anything at all – animals, objects, feelings, famous people etc.
- Explain that this activity involves thinking of the unexpected, as did the 'Tune In!' game. Give your pupils 3 minutes to work together in pairs to pair up the words so that no word is used twice and none is left over. Encourage them to be creative, to seek original connections and to be prepared to explain their reasoning.
- Invite pairs to share their best connecting idea and praise all contributions.
- Next, ask for examples of some of their 'weakest links' and encourage the rest of the class to help improve and strengthen the link by finding an alternative reason for the connection.
- Join up the pairs to make groups of 4 and give out enlarged copies of the sheet, 'Lateral Links'. Again, ask the class to generate 10 unusual nouns. These should be recorded on the sheet.
- This time, the challenge is to identify as many links as possible in 3 minutes. Whenever someone thinks of a connection, they should draw an arrow between the two words and note a brief description of the link next to it.
- Afterwards, share ideas and look for (a) the team with the most links; (b) the team with the most creative link; (c) the team with the most logical link; and (d) the team with the funniest link.

Now reflect!

Questions to consider could include:

- How did you match up the words? What methods did you use?
- What was the purpose of this activity?
- Why is it useful to learn to spot links between different words and ideas?

Keep thinking

Give your pupils two seemingly unrelated words, e.g. giraffe and igloo, and set a competition to see who can come up with the most lateral links.

Follow-up ideas

Curriculum-based lesson

'Reverse Thinking' provides an entertaining way of approaching Design and Technology projects. Brainstorming suggestions for 'how to make a useless musical instrument' or 'how to construct a bridge that won't support any weight' prompts ideas for all sorts of genuinely good methods. Alternatively, use it to approach PSHE discussions, e.g. 'What's the best way to fail an exam?' or 'What's the best way to ruin a friendship?'

'Lateral Links' is a particularly successful revision strategy as it deepens understanding and gives rise to new, previously unexplored ideas. A set of curriculum words can be generated by the class or prepared in advance by the teacher, then individuals, pairs or groups can use the sheet to record connecting ideas before sharing their favourite links. Consider turning this into a competition, with a point awarded for every connection and two points for a link that no one else thought of. An active alternative is to allocate one word to each pupil, get them to stand in a circle and throw a ball to each other, explaining the link between their words.

Examples could include:

- History – 10 words from a topic on the Egyptians, such as 'shaduf', 'pyramid', 'mummy', 'Nile', 'Pharaoh', 'Sphinx', 'hieroglyphics', 'god', 'tomb' and 'canopic jar'.
- Maths – words from a topic on shape, such as 'vertex', 'edge', 'cylinder', 'face', 'cube', 'straight', 'curved', 'two-dimensional', 'three-dimensional', 'square'.
- Science – 10 words from a topic on magnets, such as 'force', 'aluminium', 'magnetic', 'non-magnetic', 'copper', 'metal', 'push', 'pull', 'repel', 'attract', 'plastic'.

Note that the QCA schemes of work for all curriculum subjects provide a simple way of accessing and selecting key vocabulary to use for this activity (www.standards.dfes.gov.uk).

Suggestions for display

Have a 'Lateral Links' wall, with a different set of 10 word cards displayed each week. Your pupils could draw arrows between them and note the links. At the end of the week, ask them to vote for their favourite links and record these in a 'Lateral Links Log'.

Notes for use by other year groups

Increase the challenge for older pupils by giving them a blank 'Lateral Links' sheet with several arrows already marked between the boxes. Their task is to place the 10 words in such a way that the existing links can be justified, before moving on to find further connections.

Resources

Teacher instructions: **Hidden Hypotheticals**
Activity sheet: enlarged group copies of **Consider the Consequences**
Activity sheet: **Consider the Consequences** (curriculum follow-up)
You will need: plain A4 paper and masking tape

Tune in!   D C   Activity: Hidden Hypotheticals

- On the board, write the following sentence starter: 'If dogs learnt to talk, then …'
- Ask your class to suggest ways of finishing the sentence. Explain these are called 'consequences' – they are possible events that could result from the starter sentence.
- Follow the instructions provided to play the game 'Hidden Hypotheticals'.
- Afterwards, your pupils should take turns to read out their sentence starter, completed with their favourite consequence from the sheet.
- Each time, ask the class to call out whether they think that consequence is unlikely, quite likely or very likely.

Heads together

This lesson: Philosophy for Children, 'Generating the Question Session'   Page 150
Curriculum lesson: Philosophy for Children, 'Discussion Session'   Page 151
Discussion skill: Explaining ideas clearly. Encourage your class to try to express
                      their ideas and opinions as clearly as possible.

Investigate   G4   Thinking and Learning Tool: Consider the Consequences

- Explain that this activity will require your pupils to think further about predicting consequences of events. Ask them to imagine what it would be like if they could live with their friends instead of their families and get them to put up their hand if they think this idea sounds like fun. Point out that considering the consequences is valuable when making a decision, because often we rely on our instinct instead of on more careful thinking.
- Give each group an enlarged copy of the sheet 'Consider the Consequences'.
- Each group is to consider the starter sentence 'If we could live with our friends instead of our family, then …' and generate as many consequences as they can. These should be recorded in the appropriate box on their sheet.
- After 8–10 minutes, groups should consider the consequences and reach an overall decision as to whether the proposition was a good one, recording this in the box provided.
- Groups then prepare and present short plays to illustrate the possible consequences and to explain their final reasoning.

Now reflect!

Questions to consider could include:

- Can you think of decisions you might face where it would be useful to consider the consequences first?
- If you had to offer 3 pieces of advice for how to make a good decision, what would they be?
- What could be our decision-making motto for the class?

Keep thinking

If your school has a uniform, ask your pupils to consider the consequences of the following sentence: 'If we were allowed to wear whatever we wanted to school, then … ' If you have no uniform, consider the consequences of introducing one.

Follow-up ideas

Curriculum-based lesson

'Consider the Consequences' is a useful way of encouraging skills of prediction within real contexts and is developed again in Year 4, when pupils learn to ask 'What if …?' about more imaginative, unlikely situations. Begin by asking your pupils if they can remember any tips for good decision making. Why was it useful to consider the consequences of a particular action? Give each group another starter sentence, this time linked to a curriculum subject, and use the blank version of the sheet 'Consider the Consequences' to reach group decisions as to whether the proposal is a good one. Decisions can be presented as posters, plays or in discussion.

Possible ideas include:

- PSHE – If cigarettes were completely banned, then …
- Science – If we didn't do any exercise, then …
- Religious Studies – If people of different religions choose to live in separate areas, then …
- Geography – If I chose to visit a tropical/temperate country for my holiday this year, then …; If we exchanged places with children in a village in India for six months each year, then …

A useful link with a Mathematics topic on probability can also be made.

Suggestions for display

Display a different starter sentence each week – linked to curriculum topics or real life situations. Have 3 large think clouds around the sentence and a set of blank idea cards in a wall pocket. Your pupils can note their ideas and attach them to the display, before reaching a final decision.

Notes for use by other year groups

With older or more able pupils, extend the 'Consider the Consequences' activity by challenging the pupils to divide up all their 'likely' consequences into short-term, medium-term and long-term consequences.

Resources

Teacher instructions: **Visual Images**
Activity cards: two sets of the **Visual Images cards** for each pair of pupils
You will need: two trays, each with a different set of 15 objects on them, covered with cloths.

Tune in! | C | Activity: The Acrostic Game

- Share experiences of incidents when you or your pupils have been let down by mis-remembering or forgetting something. Explain that everyone can learn to improve their memory and that this lesson will introduce two useful memory methods.
- Show your class a tray covered with a cloth and give them one minute to look at the objects on the tray and remember as many as they can. Afterwards, they should make a list of those they remember before being shown the tray again.
- What methods did they use? Discuss ideas.
- Introduce acrostics as sentences where each word begins with the first letter of the object you are trying to remember. A famous one helps us remember the colours of the rainbow: **Richard** (red) **Of** (orange) **York** (yellow) **Gave** (green) **Battle** (blue) **In** (indigo) **Vain** (violet).
- Invite your pupils to invent alternative acrostic sentences for these colours.
- Finish by repeating the tray activity, this time using the acrostic method and a different set of 15 objects. Compare results.

Heads together

This lesson: Philosophy for Children, 'Generating the Question Session'   Page 150
Curriculum lesson: Philosophy for Children, 'Discussion Session'   Page 151
Discussion skill: Explaining ideas clearly. Encourage your class to try to express
                     their ideas and opinions as clearly as possible.

Investigate | G2 | D | Thinking and Learning Tool: Visual Images

- Give each pair a set of 24 'Visual Images cards' (two sets of the 12 provided) and tell them to lay them out, face down, in 6 rows of 4.
- Try Visual Images Activity One, using the instructions provided.
- After playing this once, discuss any memory strategies that your pupils used or could devise to help them. They might, for instance, try to find imaginative ways of linking the object to its position on the grid: e.g. the 3 paperclips are in the third row; the ice cream is melting and trickling out of the bottom corner etc.
- Repeat the game, encouraging your pupils to use these sorts of memory strategies.
- Next, try Visual Images Activity Two. Share some of the ideas afterwards.
- Point out that, although your class has only played this activity at a simple level, the method could be very useful if they needed to remember lots of information rather than just a few words. Strong visual images tend to stick in our minds much longer than lists of words.

You may wish to demonstrate the strength of the visual images method by asking your class if they can remember the objects from this activity several days later.

Now reflect!

Questions to consider could include:

- Can you think of any situations at home or at school when the Acrostic method or the Visual Images method might help you remember things?
- Could you invent a simple game or exercise to do each day to improve your memory? What would it be?

Keep thinking

Tell your pupils to impress their parents with their new memory skills! Get them to ask for a shopping list of 10 items, then use either the Acrostic or the Visual Images method to memorise the items.

Follow-up ideas

Curriculum-based lesson

Inventing acrostics and forming strong visual images are skills that take time and practice, so should be built into lessons wherever possible, even as a quick 5 minute activity. Examples of use include:

- Science – form visual images to remember the characteristics of different types of rocks or the function of different types of teeth.
- History – invent an acrostic to learn the stages involved at the Roman Baths or form visual images to learn the meanings of Roman words such as hypocaust, forum or basilica.
- Languages – visual images are particularly good for learning foreign vocabulary. Dr Michael Gruneberg, who formalised this method and named it the 'Link Word' technique, offers two good examples: (i) to learn that the French word for hedgehog is *'herisson'*, you could imagine that your hairy son looks like a hedgehog; (ii) to remember that *le chou* means cabbage, picture a cabbage growing out of your shoe. A useful lesson could be to give each group of pupils a list of 5 words and get them to work together to invent the strongest possible visual images to learn these words. They could draw pictures to illustrate these and present them to the rest of the class, so that, together, a large amount of vocabulary is covered.

Suggestions for display

Create a Memory Wall with examples of these two methods. Your pupils could draw pictures to record their visual links and create posters to illustrate their acrostics.

Notes for use with other year groups

Both techniques can be introduced with much younger pupils, who will benefit from learning to look out for alternative ways of making memories 'stick'. Each of the techniques introduced in Years 4, 5 and 6 rely on your pupils learning to form strong visual images.

Further resources

For further information about Dr Michael Gruneberg's resources, visit: www.linkwordlanguages.com.

List of Year 3 resources provided on the CD Rom

Lesson 1   Metacognition
> Activity sheet: **A recipe for Good Thinking and Learning**
> Teacher checklist: **20 Dispositions of an Active Thinker and Learner**

Lesson 2   Questioning
> Poster: **Remember to Ask 'Thinking Questions'**
> Activity sheet: **My Thinking Questions**

Lesson 3   Information skills
> Teacher instructions: **Tree Diagram Challenge**
> Activity cards: **Tree Diagram Challenge words**
> Activity sheet: **Tree Diagram Challenge**
> Teacher instructions: **Make your own Mind Map® and Mandala**
> Activity sheet: **Make your own Mind Map® and Mandala**

Lesson 4   Critical thinking
> Teacher instructions: **Su Doku puzzles** (2 pages)
> Activity sheet: **Su Doku puzzles**
> Activity sheet: **Define it!**

Lesson 5   Creative thinking
> Activity sheet: **Lateral Links**

Lesson 6   Decision making
> Teacher instructions: **Hidden Hypotheticals**
> Activity sheet: **Consider the Consequences**
> Activity sheet: **Consider the Consequences** (curriculum follow-up)

Lesson 7   Memory skills
> Teacher instructions: **Visual Images**
> Activity cards: **Visual Images cards**

'At a Glance' sample of Year 3 resources

These two pages show a sample selection of activity sheets for this year group. These activities and many more can be found on the CD Rom.

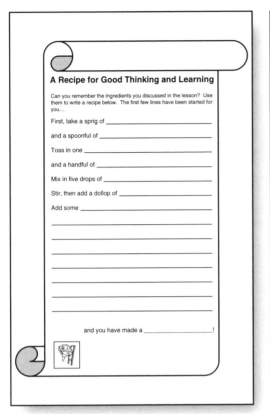

A Recipe for Good Thinking and Learning

Can you remember the ingredients you discussed in the lesson? Use them to write a recipe below. The first few lines have been started for you…

First, take a sprig of _____

and a spoonful of _____

Toss in one _____

and a handful of _____

Mix in five drops of _____

Stir, then add a dollop of _____

Add some _____

_____

_____

_____

_____

_____

and you have made a _____ !

Remember to ask 'Thinking Questions'!

'Thinking Questions' are questions that can lead to lots of different possible answers.
These questions encourage us to think more deeply about what we are learning, which can help us to understand things better.

Why do you think that …?
What do you think of …?
How could …?
What evidence do you have that …?
How many different …?
Why is …? What might …?
How do we know that …?
Can you give some reasons for …?
How can we find out if …?
What might happen if/when …?
Is it possible that …?
What if …?

Can you think of any more Thinking Questions?

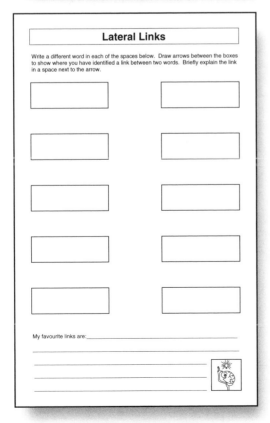

Lateral Links

Write a different word in each of the spaces below. Draw arrows between the boxes to show where you have identified a link between two words. Briefly explain the link in a space next to the arrow.

My favourite links are: _____

Visual Images cards

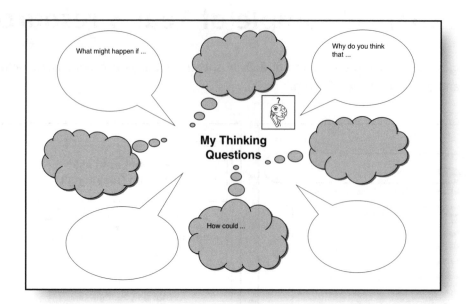

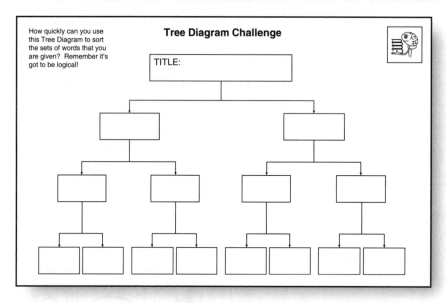

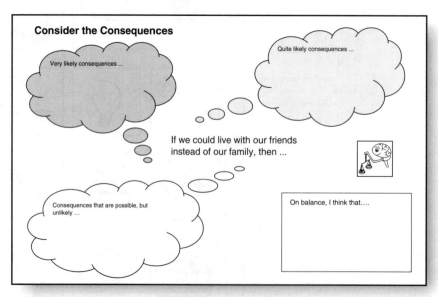

Year 4

Lesson plans and resources

Year 4 — Lesson 1

Resources

Activity cards: group sets of the **Active Thinking and Learning Dispositions cards** 🌑
You will need to find: miniature white boards or plain paper for each group

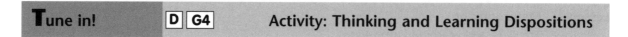

Tune in!   D G4   **Activity: Thinking and Learning Dispositions**

- Who has got any really bad habits? What is your worst habit? Do you notice when you are doing this? Is your bad habit bad for you in any way? If so, why don't you change? Use these questions and the discussion that follows to illustrate that we all have bad habits and that, once formed, they are surprisingly hard to break.
- Explain that it's just the same with thinking and learning. There are good thinking and learning habits (or 'dispositions') and bad ones. These can make a huge difference to how we get on in life, so it's important to identify any bad thinking habits that we may be forming without realising it and begin to replace these with better ones.
- Give each group a shuffled set of the 'Active Thinking and Learning Dispositions' cards. Which group can be the fastest to match up the pairs of names and descriptions of thinking and learning dispositions? Check and discuss results.

Heads together

'Heads together' Introductory session   Page 146

Investigate   D G4   **Thinking and Learning Tool: Freeze Frame**

- Allow groups to keep their full set of cards but share out the dispositions so that each group has a secret responsibility for just a few.
- Each group should put together one 'Freeze Frame' scene for each of their allocated dispositions. The scene should be silent, completely still and use all the group members. It should contain enough visual clues for the class to work out which disposition it represents.
- As each group takes their turn to present these, the watching teams should record their first, second and third guesses on paper or miniature white boards and hold these up, all at the same time. They score three points if their first guess was correct, two for their second guess and one for their third.
- Challenge the groups to sort their 20 disposition name cards into three sets: 'very important', 'quite important' and 'less important'.
- Discuss this activity. Was it difficult? If so, why? Use the discussion to illustrate the fact that it's very hard to rank the dispositions in order of importance, as much depends on what situation a person is in. Ask the groups to focus on each of the cards they were assigned and to consider the following questions:

   o Can you think of a situation where it would be *really* important to display that habit or disposition?

   o Can you think of a situation where it would *not* be at all suitable to display that particular disposition?

- Groups to present a brief summary of their discussions.

> This lesson provides an introduction to the dispositions of an active thinker and learner and will help your pupils learn what to aim for. Try to reinforce these behaviours in as many other contexts as possible, by building them into discussions, goal-setting, feedback and assessment.

Now reflect!

Questions to consider could include:

- Which dispositions do you think you are already good at?
- Which need more attention?
- Can you think of any other dispositions that should be added to the list?

Keep thinking

Invite your pupils to make a personal profile sheet, with a picture of themselves in the middle, a section for their strongest dispositions, one for those they want to work on and suitable illustrations.

Follow-up ideas

Unlike the following six lessons, there is no curriculum follow-up for the Metacognition lesson. However, you may still like to try some of the following:

 Get your class to stand up, ensuring there's plenty of space to move around. One side of the room represents 'just like me' and the other 'nothing like me'. Select a few dispositions and read these out, one at a time. Each time, your pupils should find a position in the class that reflects their own assessment of their lengths and areas for focus. This is a great activity if carried out within a supportive, humorous atmosphere. It helps to show that everyone can learn different things from each other, regardless of traditional notions of 'ability'.

- Invite your pupils to design posters to illustrate each disposition. These will serve as a useful reminder and should be referred to frequently in other lessons. For instance, ask your pupils to consider which disposition they have made most use of in a lesson or which is likely to be most valuable for the next activity. Praise them for demonstrating the dispositions on display.

Suggestions for display

Display the class posters around the room or enlarge and mount the cards provided. Ask pupils to work in pairs to add illustrations and colours to the posters to personalise the display.

Further resources

There are many excellent resources to support the development of positive thinking and learning habits. See Chapter 6 in Part One for a list of recommended books and websites.

Year 4   Lesson 2

Resources

Teacher instructions: **Things you never knew about ... Penguins**
Activity sheet: individual copies of **Things you never knew about ... Penguins**
Activity sheet: **What if?** (curriculum follow-up)
Activity sheet: **Things you never knew about ...** (curriculum follow-up)

Tune in!	C	Activity: What if? ...

- Explain that a good way to improve the creativity of our thinking is to ask, 'What if ...?'
- With your pupils standing in a circle, ask them to consider the question, 'What if ... humans were born with three legs?' and to take turns to give possible answers. Allow the option of saying 'pass'.
- Afterwards, offer those who didn't contribute another chance to do so if they wish.
- Repeat several times, with alternative 'What if ...' questions.
- The final round should give your pupils the chance to invent an apparently impossible 'What if ...' question each.

Heads together

This lesson: Philosophy for Children, 'Generating the Question Session'   Page 150
Curriculum lesson: Philosophy for Children, 'Discussion Session'   Page 151
Discussion skill: Clarifying and asking for clarification. Encourage your class to ask each other to repeat or re-phrase what they have just said if this is not clear.

Investigate	D	G2	Thinking and Learning Tool: Things you never knew about ...

- Tell your class that, when investigating a new topic, it's useful to ask questions. Ask them to imagine that they wanted to find out all about penguins. Can they think of any really interesting questions they might like to ask? List about eight of these on the board.
- Point out that, while this is a good start and these are intriguing questions, they are rather random and there is no order to them. This may mean that some important questions have been missed out. Explain that a good thinker would take this a step further by working out what *sort* of questions they might want to ask.
- Look at the list of questions. Could any be linked together into 'areas of investigation'? If so, use arrows to group the questions under suitable headings. Are there any other areas of investigation that could be added to the list? Several possible examples are provided on the instruction sheet, 'Things you never knew about ... Penguins'.
- Give out the sheet 'Things you never knew about ... Penguins'. In pairs, your pupils should complete the tree diagram to record their four chosen areas of investigation, together with three questions for each category. Encourage them to take time to think of the most interesting questions they can and emphasise that these are unlikely to be the first ones that they think of.
- Finish by inviting each pair to select their best question to read to the class.

As well as improving the quality of questioning, these activities help to show children that many things that we take for granted contain all sorts of mysteries that could be explored. Encouraging an active sense of curiosity about the world is one of the most important aims of any thinking and learning skills programme.

Now reflect!

Questions to consider could include:

- Why should we be curious about the world around us? What are the possible benefits of asking questions?
- Are there ever times when it is better not to ask questions?
- Are some questions more valuable than others? If so, what makes a good question?

Keep thinking

Your pupils might like to follow up this lesson by finding out some of the answers to their questions. An interesting website for further research is: www.adelie.pwp.blueyonder.co.uk/
The FAQs section is particularly accessible for children.

Follow-up ideas

Curriculum-based lesson

Asking 'What if ...?' encourages your pupils to be curious about the subjects they are studying and to develop skills of reasoning and hypothesising. Although the questions often seem absurd, they can also sometimes act as a creative trigger for more plausible ideas. Begin by asking your class to suggest lots of 'What if ...?' questions linked to their topic and note these on the board. Invite them to select and record 3 of these in the boxes in the middle of the 'What if ...?' sheet, using the surrounding ovals to note possible ideas. For example:

- Science – What if plants could walk? What if all liquids froze at 5°C? What if plastic conducted electricity?
- Geography – What if all forms of transport were silent? What if it was possible to recycle every single thing we used?
- History – What if the Romans had not come to England? What if we used hieroglyphics instead of our own writing system?

'Things you never knew about ...' also fits easily into schemes of work as a means of supporting investigation into a range of curriculum topics. A blank version of the sheet is provided on the CD Rom.

Suggestions for display

Ask your pupils to choose their favourite and most unusual questions about penguins, write these onto separate cards and illustrate them. Make a large tree diagram for the wall, with as many areas of investigation as are needed to classify these questions. This in itself is a useful activity and could be assigned to your more able pupils when they finish other work.

Notes for use with other year groups

Simplify the tree diagram for younger children by including just two or three areas of investigation.

Further resources

Further 'What if ...?' questions, together with other types of creative thinking activities, can be found in 'Just Suppose ...' and 'Just Suppose ... Too' by C.J. Simister, published by learn4life, www.learn4life.co.uk.

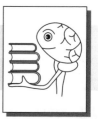

Resources

Activity cards: one set of the **Mystery Word cards**
Teacher instructions: **Diamond Ranking**
Activity cards: one set of the **Diamond Ranking cards: What makes a good discussion?**
Activity cards: group sets of the **Diamond Ranking cards: What makes a perfect school?**
Activity sheet: individual copies of **Diamond Ranking**

Tune in!	**C**	Activity: Mystery Word

- Invite one volunteer at a time to stand at the front of the class and pick a Buzz Word card.
- Their task is to describe the word without using the three other linked words that are listed.
- Repeat several times.
- Discuss what sort of skills were required to be successful at this game.

Heads together		

This lesson:	Philosophy for Children, 'Generating the Question Session'	Page 150
Curriculum lesson:	Philosophy for Children, 'Discussion Session'	Page 151
Discussion skill:	Clarifying and asking for clarification. Encourage your class to ask each other to repeat or re-phrase what they have just said if this is not clear.	

Investigate	**D** **G4**	Thinking and Learning Tool: Diamond Ranking

- Explain that we have to deal with a huge amount of information – in books, the media and the Internet – so it's useful to learn to 'prioritise' it and rank it by importance. We are also offered many different opinions, requiring us to make decisions about which ones we feel are most likely to be true.
- On the board, draw a large grid as shown on the 'Diamond Ranking cards' sheets. Show how this can be used to rank the importance of different opinions or pieces of information, so that the most important is at the top, the next two are on the second level, the least important is at the bottom and so on.
- Introduce the example: What makes a good discussion? Follow the instructions on the sheet provided.
- Give each group a set of the 'Diamond Ranking cards: What makes a perfect school?' Their task is to work together to find the best way of laying these out in a Diamond Nine pattern on their tables.
- Your pupils should use the 'Diamond Ranking' sheet to record the reasons behind their choices of most and least important option.
- Final decisions can be presented to the class, together with suggestions of further factors that could have been included in the list.

Some groups may find it difficult to work together to reach a shared decision. When difficulties arise, tell them this is a positive sign which shows they are all thinking, rather than simply copying each other. Remind them that another disposition of a good thinker is flexibility of mind – being able to alter one's opinions when new ideas come along. The activity should be used to highlight the fact that issues are rarely black and white and that a wide variety of reasoned opinions are often possible.

Now reflect!

Questions to consider could include:

- What did you think of the Diamond Ranking activity? What did it teach us?
- How well do you think your group worked together? Did you find yourself playing a particular role in the group? If so, what was it?
- Can you think of any other situations where you could use Diamond Ranking?

Keep thinking

Invite your class to make their own Mystery Word cards to be used in future lessons. Encourage them to make them as challenging as they can.

Follow-up ideas

Curriculum-based lesson

Mystery Word is an entertaining way of reinforcing the meanings of key vocabulary and it works well to invite pupils to work in pairs to produce their own sets of Mystery Word cards within a given subject.

Diamond Ranking can be applied to various curriculum subjects and the initial discussion activity leads on well to a more thoughtful follow-up task, for example:

- Geography – prioritise 9 different environmental problems, then write a letter to your local MP presenting the case for action; consider the various problems caused by too much traffic; *or* rank the importance of 9 different features of an early settlement (e.g. water supply, defence, woodland etc.) and use this to locate ideal areas on a map.
- History – decide on the order of importance of 9 different contributions that the Romans made to life today, then write and perform a documentary for a television programme.
- Art – instead of statements, your class could decide on how to rank 9 different pictures by a given artist, then make their own taped audio guide for an exhibition.

Suggestions for display

You may wish to make a set of large Diamond Nine boards, as these can be used in many different year groups and lessons. Display these around the classroom, with statements loosely attached so they can be moved around as opinions change.

Notes for use by other year groups

Adjust the level of complexity of Diamond Ranking by using 4 option cards with younger children or 16 with older pupils. Older pupils could also research different topics and devise the options themselves.

Year 4 | Lesson 4

Resources

Activity sheet: individual copies of **Alternative Explanations: I'm not so sure ...**
Activity sheet: **Alternative Explanations** (curriculum follow-up)

Tune in! | C | Activity: Picture this!

- Explain that people often 'jump to conclusions' and decide what they believe before considering all the possibilities.
- With your pupils standing in a circle, announce the first 'Picture this!' scenario: 'A circle of flattened grass has appeared in the middle of the field! What might be the reason?'
- Choose someone to start. This person should step into the circle, give a possible explanation, then point to someone else in the circle and sit down. That person should step forward, give an alternative explanation, then point to a third person and so on. Keep the atmosphere light and unthreatening. If anyone is stuck, allow them to pass until later. Continue until all are sitting down.
- Afterwards, discuss which was the most likely explanation. Which was the least likely?
- Repeat, if time, with a second 'Picture this!' scenario: 'The playground is covered with water! What might be the reason?'

Heads together

This lesson: Philosophy for Children, 'Generating the Question Session'   Page 150
Curriculum lesson: Philosophy for Children, 'Discussion Session'   Page 151
Discussion skill: Giving examples. Encourage your pupils to respond, by using the words 'For instance ...'

Investigate | D | G2 | Thinking and Learning Tool: Alternative Explanations

- Remind your class that in the 'Picture this!' scenarios it would have been easy to settle for the first explanation but, by spending time generating alternatives, they discovered that there can be lots of possible causes of an event. Point out that it is not necessarily true that the most likely one will be what really happened, as unlikely things sometimes happen too.
- The main activity develops similar skills. Give each pupil a copy of the sheet 'Alternative Explanations' and read out the first example. Generate ideas together as a class.
- Allow time for your pupils to complete the rest of the activity in pairs.
- Finish by taking each scenario at a time and sharing all the possible explanations.
- Ask your class what the purpose of this activity was. When would it be useful to think of alternative explanations?

Helpful Hints

Identifying alternative explanations is a useful way of checking the validity of a conclusion. In Critical Thinking terms, the 'post hoc' fallacy is a common error used in argument. It occurs when a claim is made that one event happened as *a result of* another previous event, purely because it happened *after* this event. Clearly, in reality there may be many alternative explanations for the second event, whose timing related to the first could be quite incidental. More able pupils may enjoy finding examples of this fallacy.

Now reflect!

Questions to consider could include:

- What types of thinking were you using for both activities (critical, analytical, creative, lateral etc.) and which dispositions would be most useful (flexibility, imagination etc.)?
- Did it become easier to think of alternative explanations as you gained more practice? If so, can you invent any games or activities to improve your thinking skills in this area?

Keep thinking

Invite your class to come up with their own 'Picture this!' scenarios.

Follow-up ideas

Curriculum-based lesson

Seeking alternative explanations within the curriculum develops your pupils' lateral thinking and their understanding that conclusions should be drawn carefully, after considering all options. Use the sheet 'Alternative Explanations' to record possible explanations. For example:

- English – relate to newspaper articles and headlines and use to illustrate that sometimes an event happens and we are too quick to assume what must have caused it. We need to stop and ask ourselves, 'Is that the most likely explanation?'
- History – give a 'silly statement' such as 'The last Romans left Britain in 410 AD. It must have been because they were fed up with the weather,' and invite your pupils to generate as many alternative explanations as they can. These can then be ranked from least to most likely.
- Geography – in a topic on water, use the sentence, 'This week, the Smith family used half as much water as they usually do. It must have been because they went out a lot.' Can your pupils think of other possible reasons?
- Science – forming hypotheses about the cause of a given observation lies at the heart of science. In a topic on friction, place a toy car at the top of a carpeted slope and invite your pupils to generate possible reasons why the car isn't moving. Alternatively, share several local, national and international environmental changes among your 'environmental consultant groups', e.g. What is causing the rise in the number of wild flowers in the United Kingdom? (The chief theory is the growing popularity of organic produce, resulting in a reduction in chemical pesticides and weedkillers.) Posters could be designed and presentations given.

Suggestions for display

 Display a 'mystery statement' on the wall each week (ideally supplied by a pupil), together with a pocket of blank think bubble clouds. Invite your pupils to fill these in, together with an illustration, whenever they think of a possible explanation and add them to the display.

Further resources

 More 'Picture this!' scenarios and other creative thinking activities are provided in 'Just Suppose ...' and 'Just Suppose ... Too', by C.J. Simister, published by learn4life, www.learn4life.co.uk.

Resources

Activity cards: group sets of the **Switch! cards**
Activity cards: one set of the **Points of View challenge cards**
Activity sheet: enlarged A3 group copies of **Points of View**
You will need to find: a whistle

Tune in! G4   Activity: Switch!

- Give each group a set of the 'Switch!' cards and turn these face down on the table.
- The first person in each group picks a card, reads it and thinks of reasons why they agree and disagree with the statement. When the whistle is blown, they should try to convince their group that the statement is a good idea.
- After 15 seconds, blow the whistle again and shout 'Switch!' The person speaking in each group should quickly switch sides and argue as convincingly as possible *against* the idea on the card. Repeat several times, varying the length of time between each change.
- Repeat the activity with the next person, who should choose a new card.

Heads together

This lesson: Philosophy for Children, 'Generating the Question Session'   Page 150
Curriculum lesson: Philosophy for Children, 'Discussion Session'   Page 151
Discussion skill: Giving examples. Encourage your pupils to respond, by using the words 'For instance ...'

Investigate D G5   Thinking and Learning Tool: Points of View

- Explain that one way to trigger new creative ideas is to put yourself in someone else's shoes and consider their perspective.
- Ask your class to imagine that they have been asked to hold a competition to raise money for a charity. Get them to call out names of famous people – past and present, real and fictional – and write these on the board. Encourage as diverse a selection as possible.
- Pick one character and get your pupils to pretend this person is faced with their task. How might they go about it? What would make the competition different and special? Discuss ideas. Point out how much more unusual and creative they are because of taking on this different point of view.
- Give each group an enlarged copy of the sheet 'Points of View' and a 'Points of View Challenge Card'. They should copy their challenge into the central rectangle, list an interesting selection of famous people in the right hand column, then find a fair way to pick four on which to focus. Record ideas for each one in a separate quadrant of the diagram.
- Allow time to prepare short presentations in which one member is the interviewer and the others take on the personalities they considered. After watching each one, the class can direct questions to any member of the group then vote on which was the best idea overall.

Encourage your class to ask the presenting group questions that probe the *process* as well as the end results of the activity, e.g. Which character helped you to come up with the most creative ideas? Why do you think that was? Was one of the characters harder than the others to 'get into'? Did that mean that the ideas were better or worse in the end?

Now reflect!

Questions to consider could include:

- What do you think of this method? Did it help you generate ideas that were more creative?
- Can you think of any situations when it might be useful to consider different points of view?
- Are there any people who have to do this particularly within their jobs?

Keep thinking

Pick a famous person and imagine the changes they might introduce in this school if they were going to be the new head teacher. On balance, do you think this would be a good thing?

Follow-up ideas

Curriculum-based lesson

In Design and Technology, the 'Points of View' activity can generate a much broader selection of possible designs than might otherwise occur. Draw up plans for a range of bridges, puppets or musical instruments, all inspired by considering other people's perspectives.

Within other subject areas, select a key question to be written in the central box. Ask your pupils to list people with a particular point of view, then select four for focus. For instance:

- History – What were the difficulties faced by people living in Roman Britain? (from the point of view of an Anglo-Saxon farmer, a Viking, a rich Roman lady, a Christian, Boudicca …).
- Geography – What should be done to improve our local area? (from the point of view of a shop keeper, a young mother, a school child, someone who is unemployed …).

Alternatively, brainstorm a range of points of view, then allocate a different person to each group of pupils. After preparation time, the group could be 'hot-seated', with the rest of the class asking questions while they speak from the viewpoint that they have researched.

Suggestions for display

Display pictures of the famous people chosen, surrounded by speech bubbles to show their ideas relating to the various challenges.

Notes for use by other year groups

With younger pupils, carry out this activity verbally, addressing a simple question such as 'What features should our new park include?' Alternatively, use an issue raised by a story as a starting point and encourage your pupils to consider the points of view of the different characters. More advanced questions can be raised with older pupils, such as 'What are the key problems for developing countries?' (from the point of view of a doctor, a farmer, an engineer, a teacher …).

Further resources

Edward de Bono's Cognitive Research Trust (CoRT) thinking tools include OPV (Other People's Views), which encourages the skills developed in this lesson. For further examples, see *CoRT1 Thinking Tools for Education* by Edward de Bono (2004). This can be purchased through Atkey Solutions at www.atkey.co.uk.

Resources

Teacher instructions: **Think 'n' Run**
Activity cards: group sets of the **Mysteries: Detective! Who is guilty? clue cards**
You will need to find: one envelope for each group

Tune in!   C   Activity: Think 'n' Run

- Your pupils should stand up, leaving plenty of space to move around.
- One end of the classroom represents 'happy' and the opposite end 'unhappy'.
- Read out the statements on the 'Think 'n' Run' instruction sheet, one by one, and ask your pupils to move into a position, somewhere between the two extremes, that represents how they feel after each statement.
- Discuss what they think the purpose of this activity was.

Heads together

This lesson: Philosophy for Children, 'Generating the Question Session'   Page 150
Curriculum lesson: Philosophy for Children, 'Discussion Session'   Page 151
Discussion skill: Asking relevant questions. Encourage your pupils to show they have listened carefully by asking questions of each other that develop the discussion.

Investigate   G4   D   Thinking and Learning Tool: Mysteries

- Tell your class they are going to be presented with a mystery to solve in groups. Read 'Setting the scene' on the sheet, 'Mysteries: Detective! Who is guilty?'.
- Give each group an envelope containing the first three clues. Do **not** tell them there is any further evidence to follow – let them assume this is the entire activity.
- Allow 3–5 minutes for the groups to read each clue in turn and to reach a shared decision about who is guilty. They are likely to find this difficult, but should be pressed to give at least a hunch as to who is responsible.
- Ask the class if they feel satisfied with their answers. Were they able to draw a conclusion that they knew was definitely true, given the available evidence? They should recognise that there was insufficient evidence to reach a firm decision.
- Explain that, on the next day of the investigation, further facts were revealed. Give each group clues 4, 5 and 6 and ask your pupils to reach a decision supported by a hypothesis about what took place. Emphasise the need to be flexible in the face of new evidence.
- After 5 minutes, ask the groups to take it in turns to give their verdict and hypothesis. How sure are they, in percentage terms, given the evidence available?
- Tell them that, on the final day of the investigation, three further clues were uncovered. Give the last three slips to each group and repeat the process. Allow time for a final discussion, then ask the groups to present their decision and supporting reasoning to the rest of the class. Are they 100% sure of their decisions now?
- Your pupils are bound to want to know the 'right answer', so you can reveal that William finally confessed. Point out that other theories were perfectly valid as, given the nine clues alone, it was not in fact possible to reach a definite decision.

Your role during the 'Mystery' activity should be to circulate, listen to conversations, support the discussion where required, but not to get involved in the decision making process. Questions such as 'How do the clues support your hypothesis?', 'Do any of the clues appear to contradict your theory?' and 'How have you had to alter your thinking so far?' are useful.

Now reflect!

Questions to consider could include:

- How did your group go about making a decision? Did you use any particular methods? (e.g. sorting the statements into piles).
- What skills (listening, reasoning, justifying, adapting …) and dispositions (collaboration, flexibility, good judgement …) did this activity require?
- How would you summarise the main purpose of this activity in one sentence?

Keep thinking

Encourage your pupils to make their own sets of 10 statements for a 'Think 'n' Run' activity.

Follow-up ideas

Curriculum-based lesson

'Think 'n' Run' is a good activity to get everyone actively involved in the decision making process. When making up a version of your own, instead of 'happy' and 'unhappy', you could set different extremes, such as 'strongly agree' and 'strongly disagree' or 'definitely' and 'never'. The theme could be linked to a historical period or event, a topical issue in the news or a moral dilemma.

When preparing a subject-based 'mystery' select a central question that has good evidence on both sides. The more ambiguous the better, as the purpose is also to show that issues are often not black and white and that there may not, in fact, be a 'right answer'. You will need to decide:

- Which central question would best suit the activity (e.g. 'Henry VIII: Good or bad?' or 'Are our weather patterns really changing?')
- How many pieces of information to give at a time.
- How to share out the information so there's a balance of evidence on both sides.
- Whether to include some 'red herrings' in the clues.

A Mathematics version can be made by setting a problem such as 'How much money will it cost to take the Adams family on holiday?', then supplying a few pieces of evidence at a time, some of which may not actually be required for the calculation.

Follow up the lesson with a written activity, as mystery activities often promote a deeper understanding of conflicting issues. For example, ask your pupils to make a list of further questions they would like to answer before they feel ready to make up their mind about the issue.

Suggestions for display

Mount the statements on separate cards on the wall, together with the question: Here is the evidence. What do *you* think?

Further resources

The 'Mysteries' thinking and learning tool, together with several other very useful strategies, is described in *Thinking through Primary Teaching* by Steve Higgins, Viv Baumfield and David Leat (2003), Chris Kington Publishing: Cambridge.

Resources

Teacher instructions: **Look, Speak, Act!**

Activity Sheet: individual copies of **Count to 10 in Spanish**

Activity cards: one set of **The Story Method: picture cards**

Tune in!	D C	Activity: Look, Speak, Act!

- Tell your class that their challenge is to learn to count to 10 in Spanish in just a few minutes.
- Discuss how your pupils normally try to learn things. Explain that learning can seem hard because we tend to use rather passive methods which don't fully activate the brain. If we can find methods that make more of our brain 'light up', there's a much greater chance that we will remember the information.
- Project the sheet 'Look, Speak, Act!' onto a large screen or give out individual copies. Follow the instructions provided.
- Afterwards, ask the class why they think this method worked so well. The key point is that it used a combination of actions, sounds and vision. The fact that the activity was unusual and funny will also make it more memorable.

Heads together

This lesson:	Philosophy for Children, 'Generating the Question Session'	Page 150
Curriculum lesson:	Philosophy for Children, 'Discussion Session'	Page 151
Discussion skill:	Asking relevant questions. Encourage your pupils to show they have listened carefully by asking questions of each other that develop the discussion.	

Investigate	C D	Thinking and Learning Tool: The Story Method

- Hold up each of the 'Story Method picture cards' for about 5 seconds and ask your pupils to remember as many as they can.
- Ask your class to share some of their earliest memories. After hearing each example, ask them why they think that particular memory has 'stuck' in their mind. List ideas on the board, for example, the incident may have been particularly funny, embarrassing, frightening etc.
- Invite your pupils to write down the cards that they can remember from the memory test earlier. Check results.
- Draw attention to the list on the board. What do all of these factors have in common? In many cases, it's likely that strong emotions were involved – whether negative or positive. Explain that the Story Method is a powerful memory technique that makes use of this discovery. It relies on the fact that humans are programmed to remember stories more easily than lists of facts. The narrative structure, imaginative content and use of humour, strong emotions and visual images all help make stories 'stick' in our minds.
- Practise the method using the picture cards provided. Show each of these for 5 seconds and encourage your pupils to form a story in their mind that links the images. Remind them that the funnier, the more vivid, absurd or embarrassing, the better.

- Before getting your pupils to write a list of the words they can remember, ask them to stand up and recite the numbers 1 to 10 in Spanish again, using the method learnt earlier.
- Finish by comparing results: did the story method help them to improve their word score?

> Another strength of the Story Method is that it allows the user to remember words (and therefore, ideas and concepts) in a particular order. This can be valuable in some contexts.

Now reflect!

Questions to consider could include:

- How good do you think your memory normally is?
- Is it better for some things than others?
- When might you be able to use the Story Method to make learning easier?

Keep thinking

Tell your class that teaching other people is a good way of remembering and learning new things. Encourage them to teach someone at home how to count to 10 in Spanish. If they are learning other languages, can they work out similar methods for learning their numbers?

Follow-up ideas

Curriculum-based lesson

As with all memory devices, the Story Method requires significant practice to become a familiar tool. Your pupils are likely to struggle initially to find suitable contexts for it themselves, so help them by supplying examples across the curriculum. Where words do not immediately lend themselves to items in a story, your pupils will need to be more creative in turning them into visual images. For example:

- Science – develop stories to learn the correct order of the planets traditionally listed in the Solar System, e.g.:

  The **Sun** was feeling unwell one day so decided to take his temperature. Unfortunately, the thermometer broke and **Mercury** trickled out. The Sun was so hot and bothered that the veins (**Venus**) on his temples bulged and he stamped around, making a huge mess (**Mars**). 'By **Jupiter**!' he shouted, and sat (**Saturn**) down, exhausted. Just then, it began to rain (**Uranus**), which cooled the Sun down a little and made him feel better. He began to hum a little tune (**Neptune**) and out popped his dog, **Pluto**, very glad to see him looking more cheerful at last.
- History – learn the order of Henry VIII's wives or of a series of monarchs within a given period.
- Geography – make up a story to learn the names of the biggest rivers or mountains in a country.
- Religious Studies – use the Story Method to remember the main features of a building of worship or of a particular faith.

Suggestions for display

Create a display that reminds your pupils of the processes involved in the Story Method by asking them to draw cartoon pictures to illustrate the different stages of their stories, with the events described below and the key words highlighted.

Further resources

To find out more about a range of memory methods, try *Use Your Memory* by Tony Buzan (2003), London: BBC Worldwide Limited.

List of Year 4 resources provided on the CD Rom

Lesson 1   Metacognition
    Activity cards: **Active Thinking and Learning Dispositions cards** (3 pages)

Lesson 2   Questioning
    Teacher instructions: **Things you never knew about ... Penguins**
    Activity sheet: **Things you never knew about ... Penguins**
    Activity sheet: **What if?** (curriculum follow-up)
    Activity sheet: **Things you never knew about ...** (curriculum follow-up)

Lesson 3   Information skills
    Activity cards: **Mystery Word cards** (2 pages)
    Teacher instructions: **Diamond Ranking**
    Activity cards: **Diamond Ranking cards: What makes a good discussion?**
    Activity cards: **Diamond Ranking cards: What makes a perfect school?**
    Activity sheet: **Diamond Ranking**

Lesson 4   Critical thinking
    Activity sheet: **Alternative Explanations: I'm not so sure ...**
    Activity sheet: **Alternative Explanations** (curriculum follow-up)

Lesson 5   Creative thinking
    Activity cards: **Switch! cards**
    Activity cards: **Points of View challenge cards**
    Activity sheet: **Points of View**

Lesson 6   Decision making
    Teacher instructions: **Think 'n' Run**
    Activity cards: **Mysteries: Detective! Who is guilty?** (2 pages)

Lesson 7   Memory skills
    Teacher instructions: **Look, Speak, Act!**
    Activity sheet: **Count to 10 in Spanish**
    Activity cards: **The Story Method picture cards** (8 pages)

'At a Glance' sample of Year 4 resources

These two pages show a sample selection of activity sheets for this year group. These activities and many more can be found on the CD Rom.

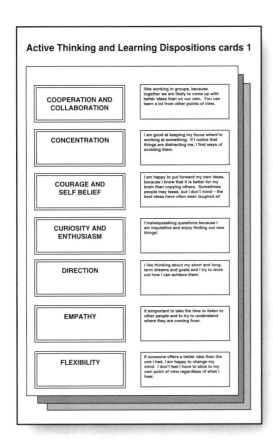

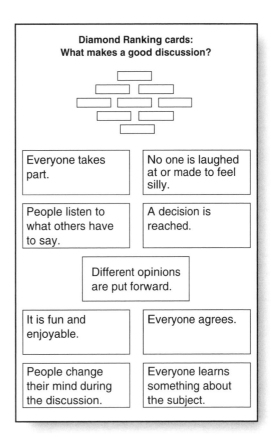

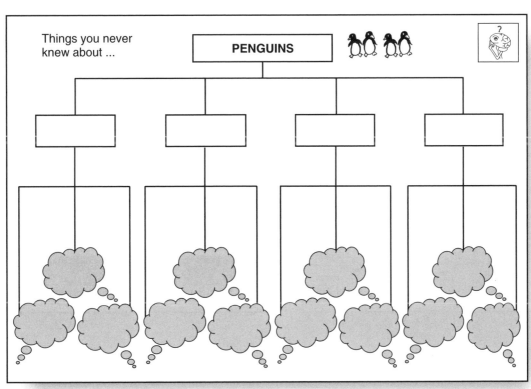

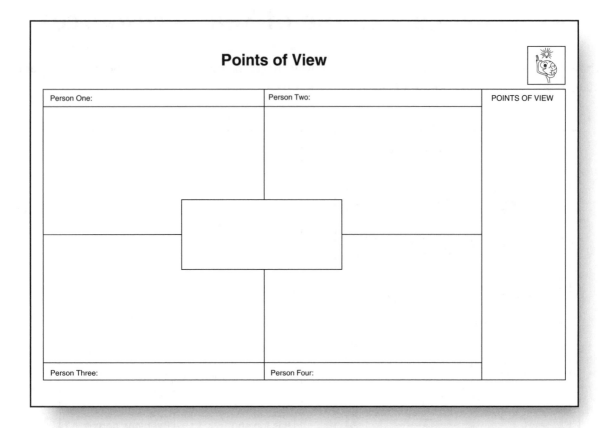

Points of View

POINTS OF VIEW

Person One:

Person Two:

Person Three:

Person Four:

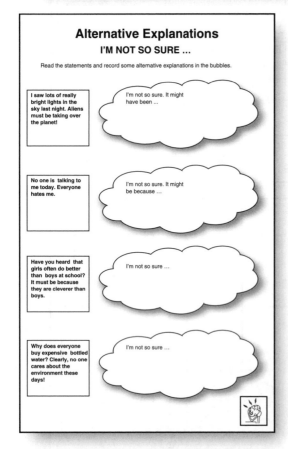

Alternative Explanations

I'M NOT SO SURE ...

Read the statements and record some alternative explanations in the bubbles.

I saw lots of really bright lights in the sky last night. Aliens must be taking over the planet!

I'm not so sure. It might have been ...

No one is talking to me today. Everyone hates me.

I'm not so sure. It might be because ...

Have you heard that girls often do better than boys at school? It must be because they are cleverer than boys.

I'm not so sure ...

Why does everyone buy expensive bottled water? Clearly, no one cares about the environment these days!

I'm not so sure ...

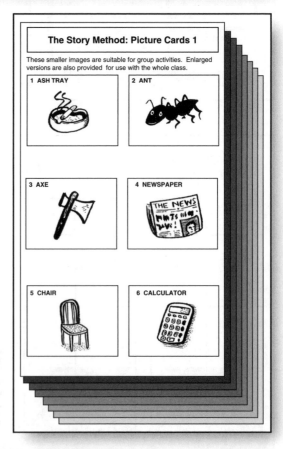

The Story Method: Picture Cards 1

These smaller images are suitable for group activities. Enlarged versions are also provided for use with the whole class.

1 ASH TRAY

2 ANT

3 AXE

4 NEWSPAPER

5 CHAIR

6 CALCULATOR

Lesson Plans and Resources

Lesson 1   Metacognition
My Amazing Brain
Learning Styles

Lesson 2   Questioning
Catch me if you can!
What's the question?

Lesson 3   Information skills
Word Links
Be a Thinking Detective!

Lesson 4   Critical thinking
Disconnect!
Cause and Effect: Multi-Flow Maps

Lesson 5   Creative thinking
The Problem Game
Improve it!

Lesson 6   Decision Making
What could it be?
Reflective Decision Making

Lesson 7   Memory Skills
Break up!
The Journey Method

List of resources provided on the CD Rom

'At a Glance' sample of resources

Year 5   Lesson 1

Resources

Activity sheet: individual copies of **My Amazing Brain**
Teacher instructions: **Learning Styles**
Activity cards: group sets of the **Learning Styles: I could try … cards**
Activity sheet: individual copies of **My brain and how it learns best**
You will need to find: a large sheet of paper for each group.

Tune in!	D I	Activity: My Amazing Brain

- Ask your pupils who thinks they have an amazing brain. Use this as an opportunity to explain that they *all* have amazing brains: every minute of the day and night, their brains are busy, doing and thinking all sorts of things, many of which they don't even notice.
- Invite ideas from your pupils about what the brain does. Discuss some of the mechanical functions it controls (e.g. our breathing, our sight, our hearing) and the intellectual functions it controls (e.g. our memory, our ideas, our likes and dislikes, our emotions).
- Explain that it can help us to understand our complicated brains if we compare them to something else. Think of your brain, for example, as a house, with lots of rooms, each full of the things needed for a different task that the brain does. What might be in the memory room? The taste room? The emotions room?
- Can your pupils think of any other brain analogies? They might make comparisons with computers, sets of art equipment, jungles full of different plants and animals, a circus complete with animals, clowns and acrobat … Probe each idea to develop the analogy.
- Favourite ideas should be selected and drawn on the outline sheet 'My Amazing Brain'.
- Allow time at the end for discussing the different analogies.

Heads together

'Heads together' Introductory session   Page 146

Investigate	D G4 I	Thinking and Learning Tool: Learning Styles

- Follow the instructions 'Learning Styles' provided.
- Display the Venn Diagrams around the room and invite your pupils to walk around, look at each one in turn and try to decide whether the methods that most appeal to them are visual, auditory or kinaesthetic. Which methods appeal least?
- Give your pupils a copy of the activity sheet 'My brain and how it learns best'. Allow time for them to complete each section, using a photograph or drawing a picture for the central circle.

Our understanding of the brain is changing all the time with the result that new facts and approaches can quickly become discredited, so this introduction to learning styles is deliberately very general. It is far too simplistic to try to classify complex human brains into three clear 'types'. However, it does seem likely that we learn in different ways – that we have varying 'learning preferences'. It's important, therefore, to give children the chance to think about their own personalities, to explore as many of these different learning methods as possible and to discover which ones will prove most effective for them.

Now reflect!

Questions to consider could include:

- Why do you think we did these activities?
- Have you discovered anything new about yourself? Do you seem more likely to prefer visual, auditory, kinaesthetic or a mixture of these methods?
- When might you be able to try out these new methods? Which will you try first?

Keep thinking

Ask your pupils to think of three more learning methods to add to the Venn Diagrams.

Follow-up ideas

Unlike the following six lessons, there is no curriculum follow-up for the Metacognition lesson. However, you may still like to try some of the following:

- As this was a very general introduction to different ways of learning, you may like to give your pupils the chance to try out a questionnaire to help them reflect on their learning preferences. Various options are available online.
- Transfer all the ideas from the Venn Diagrams, including extra methods your pupils think of, onto one class diagram. Send copies of this to parents, as a guide for how to help their children when learning and revising at home.
- Discuss the following quote: 'The greatest unexplored territory in the world is the space between your ears' – Bill O'Brien. What do your pupils think this means? What implications could it have for the way we live our lives?

Suggestions for display

 Display the Venn Diagrams as a reminder of the range of learning methods to be explored.

Further resources

Bill O'Brien is quoted in *The Learning Revolution: To Change the Way the World Learns* (2001) by Gordon Dryden and Jeanette Vos, Network Educational Press Ltd, Visions of Education series, p. 143.

Resources

Teacher instructions and sample questions: **Catch me if you can** 🌐
Activity cards: one set of **Catch me if you can! Person X and Person Y cards** 🌐
Activity sheet: individual copies of **What's the question?** 🌐
Activity sheet: **What's the question?** (curriculum follow-up) 🌐
You will need to find: plain paper

Tune in!　D A　Activity: Catch me if you can!

- It takes time to get used to the rules of this game but, once familiar, it's extremely popular and much quicker to play. The first time may take about 20 or 30 minutes.
- Explain that two teams will compete to catch each other's 'mystery person'. This is done by asking questions to discover all the other team's information. The information that needs to be discovered is the mystery person's name, age, country, job, favourite food, favourite hobby and pet.
- Divide your class into teams, then follow the instructions provided.

Heads together

This lesson:　　　Philosophy for Children, 'Generating the Question Session'　　Page 150
Curriculum lesson:　Philosophy for Children, 'Discussion Session'　　　　　　　Page 151
Discussion skill:　　Quoting or paraphrasing what others have said. Encourage your class to re-tell the main points that other people have made, to ensure understanding, for example: 'What X is saying is ...'

Investigate　　D A I　Thinking and Learning Tool: What's the question?

- Write the word 'elephant' on the board.
- Tell your pupils that, whereas normally in school they are given questions and asked to find answers, for this activity the opposite is true. The word 'elephant' is the answer. What might be the question? Encourage as many answers as possible.
- Raise the level of challenge by asking for questions where the word 'elephant' is the *only* possible answer.
- Give each pupil a piece of plain paper and invite them to write a one-word answer on it, then screw it up into a ball. On the count of three, they should all throw these across the room in any direction, then pick up whichever ball they want. They then have 15 seconds to write down a question for which that word is the answer, before screwing up the paper and throwing it across the room again. Repeat several times, then return the pieces of paper to their owners. Finish by asking everyone to share their favourite question from their sheet.
- Consolidate with activity sheet 'What's the question?'

Your pupils are likely to find it quite challenging to come up with a question that can *only* lead to a specific given answer and this should prompt an interesting debate. When suggestions are given, turn them around and ask the class whether they can think of any way of answering that question other than the given option

Now reflect!

Questions to consider could include:

- Why do you think you played 'Catch me if you can?'
- What skills did it develop? (e.g. listening, creative thinking to generate the clues, deduction to make use of the clues).
- What skills did you need for 'What's the question?'.

Keep thinking

Ask your pupils to make their own answer sheets for a 'What's the question?' activity and use these as warm-ups in other lessons. Alternatively, choose a different child each day to think of and write an answer on the board. At the end of the day, the class could suggest possible questions that 'fit' it.

Follow-up ideas

Curriculum-based lesson

'What's the question?' is an easy strategy to apply to the curriculum and is useful in two ways:

- To clarify understanding of key vocabulary within different subjects. Repeat the activity described, with pupils throwing balls of paper across the class and listing as many questions as they can for each answer. Alternatively, use the sheet 'What's the question' to list important words and ask your pupils to think of questions that could only lead to these given answers. Encourage creative thinking with a few less obvious answers such as 'it was difficult' or 'hardly ever' and see if your pupils can fit answers to these that relate to the topic you are discussing!
- To improve comprehension skills – give your pupils a piece of fiction or non-fiction text, together with a series of 'answers', ranging from simple one-word answers to longer phrases, where more complex questions need to be found. This activity is particularly good for pupils to work on in pairs, as discussion is likely to improve the precision of the questions that are generated. Encourage your class to think of questions that are as interesting and thoughtful as possible.

Suggestions for display

Neither activity leads to an obvious display in this case, though you may like to have an 'Answer of the Day' corner, where you note your pupils' chosen word each day (see the 'Keep thinking' activity).

Notes for use by other year groups

'Catch me if you can!' is quite a complicated game, so is best suited to pupils in Years 5 and 6. More able pupils may like to research facts about famous people and play a 'Catch me if you can – Celebrity!' version of the game.

'What's the question?' can be used with all ages by adjusting the level of complexity and number of the answers provided.

Resources

Teacher instructions: **Be a Thinking Detective!** (2 pages) 🌐
Activity sheet: enlarged group copies of **Be a Thinking Detective!** (2 pages) 🌐
Activity sheet: group copies of **Witness Statements** 🌐
Activity sheet: enlarged group copies of **Crime Hypothesis** 🌐
You will need to find: an individual white board, pen and wiper for each group and the resources listed on the instruction sheet

Tune in!	G6	**Activity: Word Links**

- Ask your class to call out 12 words linked with the word 'aliens'. Write these on the board.
- Give each team an individual white board, pen and wiper (or paper). Allow one minute for each of the following tasks:
  - Draw a diagram or concept map showing as many links as possible between the 12 words – write a 3 or 4 word explanation along each connecting line.
  - With the words in the reverse order to that written on the board, put them into sentences using the smallest number of total words possible.
  - Sort the words into 3 groups of 4 and give a logical rationale for your decision.
  - Find a way of linking all 12 words in just one sentence.
  - Find a way of linking all 12 words to make the shortest logical paragraph possible.
- Between each task, ask the groups to show or read out their 'solution' and award 3 points if they have done very well, 2 points for a good effort and 1 point for an attempt of some sort.
- At the end, count up points to find the Word Links winner.

Heads together

This lesson:	Philosophy for Children, 'Generating the Question Session'	Page 150
Curriculum lesson:	Philosophy for Children, 'Discussion Session'	Page 151
Discussion skill:	Quoting or paraphrasing what others have said. Encourage your class to re-tell the main points that other people have made, to ensure understanding, for example: 'What X is saying is ...'	

Investigate	G4	**Thinking and Learning Tool: Be a Thinking Detective!**

- This activity takes about 45 minutes and could be spread over 2 sessions.
- Explain that finding out about a new topic is rather like being a detective. Instead of simply copying everything you discover from books or the Internet etc., research should be an interesting and active process.
- Follow the 'Be a Thinking Detective!' instructions to work through the steps involved.

The purpose of this activity is to:
* raise your pupils' enthusiasm for investigative research
* encourage them to take more responsibility for directing their own learning
* emphasise the importance of thinking actively about what they discover

It is important therefore to make the links with 'real life' study as explicit as you can at each stage of the process. You are hoping to replace the 'copying habit' with the following steps:
1. Choosing and defining your aim   2. Asking questions   3. Planning   4. Gathering information
5. Thinking critically and creatively   6. Fitting the pieces together

Now reflect!

Questions to consider could include:
* Why do you think we did this activity? What did it teach us?
* In what other situations would it be useful to be Thinking Detectives?
* How well do you think your group worked together? What was good? What could have been improved?

Keep thinking

Ask your pupils to draw and label their own bag of evidence for a crime. These could be presented to the class, who should come up with quick deductions about what they might reveal.

Follow-up ideas

Curriculum-based lesson

Word Links is an excellent way of reinforcing understanding within the curriculum. Get your pupils to generate 12 words linked with your topic, then work in pairs rather than larger groups, so everyone is involved. Use the final challenge to illustrate the skills needed to write clear explanatory paragraphs.

Use the 'Be a Thinking Detective!' sheet to guide small groups of pupils in the process of investigating a new topic. Within your given topic, allow them to select questions that *they* are interested in pursuing so they have ownership of the project. Set up a 'research circus', with a wide range of resources (books, CD Roms, audio CDs, posters etc.) at different points around the room, and allow groups time to move from one to the other, as well as to use the school library and the Internet. Emphasise the importance of Step 5 – your pupils should be learning to be selective, to include only the information that they feel has most value, and to add their own ideas rather than just repeating those of other people.

A great extension activity makes use of the 'Expert Method'. Once each group has carried out their investigation into a given area, they should teach this to the rest of the class, perhaps by preparing a short presentation or play. A more challenging version of this – the 'Jigsaw Method' – is usually more suitable for older pupils but can be carried out with younger children, providing sufficient support is given. This involves taking the initial 'expert groups' and forming new mixed groups with one expert from each area. These new 'jigsaw groups' are set a collaborative task that requires each of their expert knowledge, e.g. designing a board game that illustrates all the different researched components of the topic or making a class magazine or poster.

Suggestions for display

Who dunnit? Display the artists' impressions of the mystery person, along with group hypotheses and the original witness statements. Include questions such as: Which picture do *you* think fits the descriptions best? Which hypothesis is most imaginative? Which is most logical? Report back if you have any more ideas about this crime.

<table>
<tr><td>

Year 5

</td><td>

Lesson 4

</td><td>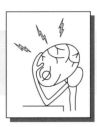</td></tr>
</table>

Resources

Activity sheet: Enlarged group copies of **Cause and Effect: Multi-Flow Map** 💿
Activity cards: One set of **Cause and Effect cards** 💿
Activity sheet: **Cause and Effect: Multi-Flow Map** (for younger pupils) 💿

Tune in!   [C]   **Activity: Disconnect!**

- With your pupils standing in a circle, ask someone to suggest any word that comes into their head.
- Who thinks they can come up with a word that is not in any way related to this starter word? Do the others agree? Can anyone challenge this person by finding a logical connection between the two words?
- Explain that the object of the game is to take turns to say a word that's completely unconnected to the previous word. If anyone spots a connection, they should call 'Challenge!' and explain their idea.
- A player must sit down if they:
  - Take longer than 5 seconds to state their word
  - Are correctly challenged by someone else before the next person has given their word

---

Heads together

This lesson: Philosophy for Children, 'Generating the Question Session'   Page 150
Curriculum lesson: Philosophy for Children, 'Discussion Session'   Page 151
Discussion skill: Building on what others have said. Encourage your class to refer to what others have said and occasionally to summarise the progress of the discussion.

Investigate   [D] [G4]   **Thinking and Learning Tool:** **Cause and Effect: Multi-Flow Map**

- Stand on a chair in front of the class. Ask your pupils to think of as many reasons as they can for why you might be doing this. Encourage them to be as imaginative as possible. Then ask them to describe what effect your action had on them.
- Explain that analysing the causes and effects of an event is a good way to understand it more deeply. In the middle of the board, draw a square and write the word 'Event' in it. Ask your class what sort of diagram might be useful to record causes and effects of an event. They may well reach a decision that's similar to the diagram on the 'Cause and Effect: Multi-Flow Map' sheet provided, in which case praise them for their good logical thinking.
- Give each group a copy of the sheet and a 'Cause and Effect' card. Their task is to work together to record as many causes and effects as they can for this particular event, adding further boxes if they wish.
- Afterwards, each group should present their analysis to the class in a style of their choosing, for example by acting out the possible causes and effects.

If you'd prefer not to stand on a chair, do something else surprising, such as lying on the ground or balancing an apple on your head!

Now reflect!

Questions to consider could include:

- In what situations is it a good idea to consider the causes and effects?
- In which school subjects might this be particularly useful?
- What sort of thinking skills were you using for this activity?

Keep thinking

Set a 'thinking homework' task: What might be the causes and effects of having no homework tonight?

Follow-up ideas

Curriculum-based lesson

Multi-Flow Maps can be used in several subjects, for example:

- Geography – they would suit environmental topics (e.g. The Arctic ice caps are melting); studies of a location (e.g. The local post office is closing); and could be used to analyse trends (e.g. The number of people living in villages is increasing again after a long-term decline). Placing photographs in the central box is another great activity.
- History – to encourage a deeper understanding of important events and changes.
- English – within character analysis, to investigate motivations and consequences of actions; or to investigate topical events, by considering a range of newspaper headlines and pictures.
- PSHE – to develop empathy in understanding another person's actions.

Increase the challenge for more able pupils, by allowing them to select any of the causes they have identified and consider what caused these to happen. Similarly, the diagram can be extended to the right by focusing on one of the identified effects and considering what its effects might be.

Suggestions for display

 Create a 'Cause and Effect Corner', with an enlarged copy of the Multi-Flow Map. Enter a different event each week for your pupils to think about. Mount headlines and pictures from newspapers for pupils to analyse using this technique.

Notes for use by other year groups

A simpler version of the 'Cause and Effect: Multi-Flow Map' with just three boxes on each side can be used for younger children. (This is included on the CD Rom.)

Further resources

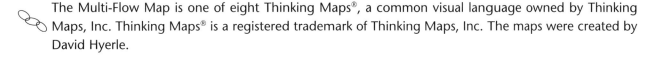 Disconnect! can be found in Robert Fisher's very useful book *Games for Thinking* (where it is called 'Random Words'), published by Nash Pollock Publishing, 1997.

The Multi-Flow Map is one of eight Thinking Maps®, a common visual language owned by Thinking Maps, Inc. Thinking Maps® is a registered trademark of Thinking Maps, Inc. The maps were created by David Hyerle.

Resources

Activity sheet: individual copies of **Improve it: Objects**

Activity sheet: **Improve it: Situations** (curriculum follow-up)

You will need to find: an elastic band and a mobile phone

Tune in! | **C** | **Activity: The Problem Game**

- Ask your pupils to stand in a circle. Show them an elastic band and tell them that, although it's quite useful, its problem is that it won't stretch enough to go around a big pile of books.
- Pass the elastic band around the circle. Pupils should take turns to come up with other inventive ways to complete the sentence, 'The problem with this elastic band is that …', e.g. … it's a boring colour; … it doesn't smell very nice; … it would hurt if you wore it as a bracelet; … you couldn't use it to catapult an elephant over a fence …
- Which of these problems could usefully be solved? Could identifying problems lead to some genuine improvements in the design of the elastic band?
- Point out that this is often where inventions come from: by questioning everyday things, identifying problems instead of just accepting them and considering how they could be solved.

Heads together

This lesson: Philosophy for Children, 'Generating the Question Session'   Page 150

Curriculum lesson: Philosophy for Children, 'Discussion Session'   Page 151

Discussion skill: Building on what others have said. Encourage your class to refer to what others have said and occasionally to summarise the progress of the discussion.

Investigate | **G2** | **I** | **Thinking and Learning Tool: Improve it!**

- Hold up a mobile phone and ask your pupils to describe its features. Point out how much phones have changed since they were first invented. Improving them has become an important business.
- Allow 2 minutes for your pupils in pairs to think of special features for the next generation of mobile phones. Encourage them to be imaginative but also to think of realistic ideas.
- Share ideas. You might want to tell them that one company has invented a mobile phone that helps people with their golf swing!
- Now get them to close their eyes and visualise walking around their house to look for other everyday objects that could be improved. They should select one and use the sheet 'Improve it!' to:
  o Note the characteristics of the object as it is now: e.g. size, colour, shape, material, special features etc.
  o Brainstorm ideas for how they could improve these characteristics using the think bubbles underneath
  o Select the best combination of ideas to describe and draw their new invention in the box at the bottom.
- Pause the activity after 5 minutes and encourage your pupils to pair up, tell each other about their ideas and offer suggestions to help make them even better.
- Your pupils should prepare and present a 15 second advertisement to 'sell' their inventions to the rest of the class.

The main purpose of this activity is to teach pupils that good ideas rarely come out of nowhere. Instead, they are often simply a new combination of old ideas or an improvement on something that already exists. An interesting discussion is generated by asking your class to think of any modern invention that *isn't* a development of something previously in existence. Your aim is to encourage them to recognise that inventing should not be something that's left to other people – we can all be inventors and creators of new and improved ideas.

Now reflect!

Questions to consider could include:

- Do you think the world needs inventors? Why?
- What have you learnt about inventing?
- What do you think of the ideas that you generated? If you could pick one that you think really could be successful, which would it be?

Keep thinking

Encourage your class to look out for things that could be improved in the world around them – either in their everyday situations, or at a local, national or even international level. Note these 'problems' on cards and display them under the title 'Year 5: Improvement Consultants!'. Supply plenty of self-adhesive notes so your pupils can jot down solutions and stick these around the cards on the display.

Follow-up ideas

Curriculum-based lesson

Remind pupils that good creative thinkers question everyday things, identify problems and use their imaginations to solve them rather than simply accepting things as they are. This also applies to situations and ideas: creative thinkers ask 'How could this situation be improved?' and 'How might that problem have been solved in a different way?'

Select a problem issue to consider within a curriculum subject and invite your pupils to act as 'Improvement Consultants', using the sheet 'Improve it!' to analyse the situation and offer ideas, e.g.

- Geography – poverty in less developed countries (characteristics could include unequal distribution of wealth, limited food supply, unsafe water supply, lack of sufficient medicine, disease, poor transport and infrastructure etc.); the local high street (characteristics could include congestion, limited parking, litter etc.).
- History – the treatment of the Aztecs (characteristics could include lack of respect for religion, introduction of Western diseases, stealing their property etc.); the situation for poor children in Victorian times (characteristics could include limited education, poor hygiene, few rights etc.). Each group could prepare a presentation of their ideas to show the class.

Suggestions for display

 See 'Keep Thinking'.

Notes for use by other year groups

With younger pupils, simplify this activity by giving them a picture of an everyday object and asking them to surround it with all their ideas for improvements. They can present these to the class, picking out their favourite suggestions.

Resources

Activity sheet: individual copies of **What could it be?**
Activity sheet: individual copies of **Reflective Decision Making**
Activity cards: one set of the **Reflective Decision Making cards**

| **T**une In! | **C** | **Activity: What could it be?** |

- Explain that good decision making involves creative thinking, as generating lots of imaginative options nearly always results in a better decision.
- Give out individual copies of the sheet 'What could it be?'
- Allow 3 to 5 minutes for pupils to complete the sheet by turning the circles into anything they wish. Explain that they will get 1 point for each idea and 2 points for any that are unique to them.
- Share ideas and award points. Finish by asking your pupils to decide which was their best idea.

Heads together

This lesson: Philosophy for Children, 'Generating the Question Session'   Page 150
Curriculum lesson: Philosophy for Children, 'Discussion Session'   Page 151
Discussion skill: Being concise. Encourage your class to avoid diversion and to try to keep their focus on the question at hand and on what has just been said.

Investigate   **C** **G2** Thinking and Learning Tool: Reflective Decision Making

- Ask your pupils what they would choose if they could have any car in the world. Gather ideas, then ask how they made the decision. What factors did they take into account? Did they consider the purpose of the car (e.g. whether for the whole family or just them), the practicality of the car (e.g. running costs, whether it would fit in the garage, if it's a reliable make) or just the appearance and speed?
- Point out that we often rely on 'instinct' when making a decision and, while this is sometimes successful, it may mean we make decisions that fail to take into account all the factors. Ask what steps could be taken when making an important decision and discuss ideas, e.g.
  o Is there anything I need to find out or take into account before I even consider the decision? (e.g. size of garage, budget etc.)
  o What are all the possible options available to me?
  o What are the pros and cons of the different options?
  o What might their consequences be?
  o Which is the best decision on balance?
- Give each group a Reflective Decision Making card and give the sheet 'Reflective Decision Making' to each pupil. Explain the stages on the sheet, then allow time for them to work

through the activity and reach a final decision. Suggest suitable sentence starters such as 'Overall, I think that ...' and 'On balance, I have decided that ...'

- Groups should finish by reading out their card to the class, presenting their final decision and explaining their reasoning.

You may need to help groups with the first stage of the 'Reflective Decision Making' sheet. For example, the group considering where they'd take a trip on a magic carpet might consider whether any of the group get travel sickness, which languages they speak between them and whether they'd need more money to enjoy some places more than others.

Now reflect!

Questions to consider could include:

- If you had to sum up the main point of this session, what do you think it would be?
- Can you think of any really important decisions you have had to make?
- How could these steps apply?

Keep thinking

Get your pupils to think of more imaginary decisions of the type used in the 'Reflective Decision Making' activity. Choose one each day and write it on the board for everyone to consider.

Follow-up ideas

The 'What could it be?' activity can be repeated by making a second sheet with squares or with circles containing a smaller circle inside them.

The same 'Reflective Decision Making' sheet can be used within curriculum subject decisions. For example:

- History – What should Elizabeth I do about Mary Queen of Scots? If I lived in Greek times, what would I find hardest to deal with? If I were an Aztec, what hobby/job would I most like to have?
- English – pupils could put themselves in the position of a character in the class reader and consider a difficult decision they are facing.
- Geography – What is the most important thing we could do to improve the school environment? What one new law could be introduced to help the environment?
- PSHE – if you were offered a cigarette, what would you do? If you knew your best friend had stolen something, what would you do?

Depending on the context, you may need to provide research resources to support the activity. It is useful to follow up with a written activity of some type, such as a letter to Queen Elizabeth I from one of her chief advisers or a diary entry for a book character.

Suggestions for display

Divide your class into five groups and give each group one of the decision making steps described in the lesson. Their task is to produce a poster to illustrate this step, so that together they create a display that covers all the stages.

Further resources

The 'What could it be?' activity can be found on p. 38 of Robert Fisher's book *Teaching Children to Think* (2nd edn, 2005), London: Nelson Thornes.

Year 5 — Lesson 7

Resources

Activity sheet: enlarged group copies of **The Journey Method: Shopping List**

Tune in! |C| **Activity: Break up!**

- Divide your class into 3 teams: A, B and C. During the game, the teams will rotate through 3 different roles: Arrangers, Models and Observers.
- The Observers rest their heads on their desks so they can't see what's happening. Meanwhile, the Arrangers 'place' the Models in positions of their choice – either to make a group scene or with individuals scattered in random positions.
- The Observers are then given 10 seconds to wander around and look at the Models, before the Arrangers shout 'Break up!' and the Models return to their seats.
- The Observers must then place the Models in the positions they remember. A point is gained for each person correctly placed.
- Repeat so each team has at least one turn in each role. Afterwards, discuss tactics and methods that your pupils devised to gain more points.

Heads together

This lesson: Philosophy for Children, 'Generating the Question Session' Page 150
Curriculum lesson: Philosophy for Children, 'Discussion Session' Page 151
Discussion skill: Being concise. Encourage your class to avoid diversion and to try to keep their focus on the question at hand and on what has just been said.

Investigate |D| |G4| **Thinking and Learning Tool: The Journey Method**

- Explain that trying to hold lots of items in the short-term memory is an unreliable way of remembering them. A better method is to hook new memories onto old ones that are already in our much bigger long-term memory bank. Some things are so thoroughly stored there we are unlikely ever to forget them, e.g. how often do we forget where our bedroom is? Who can remember not only where the rooms are in their house, but exactly what each room looks like? Point out that visual images are particularly memorable – as was seen in the 'Break up!' game.
- Ask your pupils to close their eyes and visualise walking around their own home. Imagine knocking at the front door. As they enter, what's the first place they come to? A hall? A living room? Encourage them to picture it as clearly as they can. What about the next room? Get them to take a few moments to picture the most obvious route around their home, then write a list of the 10 places they visited, in order. Encourage them to fix this journey in their mind.
- Give each group a copy of the shopping list. The Journey Method involves them taking each item on the list, one at a time, and picturing it in a room of their house. The funnier or sillier the image, the more likely it will stick, so encourage them to be imaginative. For instance, they might picture the first item – bread – squashed and sticking through the letter box of their front door.
- Allow time for your pupils to work individually on their memory journeys, then to pair up and tell each other about the images they pictured.
- Finish by asking your class to write down – from memory – the items on the shopping list.

For longer lists, your pupils could picture 2 or 3 objects in each room or select an alternative journey that they know well, such as the one from home to school. You could choose a familiar route around the school and reinforce this by walking around this route and drawing attention to the key places. This same journey can then be used by everyone to help learn information from a wide range of subjects.

Now reflect!

Questions to consider could include:

- Can you think of situations where you need to remember a list of words or pieces of information? Could the Journey Method help?
- What are the strengths and weaknesses of the Journey Method?

Keep thinking

Ask your pupils to call out random words that come into their heads and write 30 of these in a spare space on the board. Who can be crowned memory champion of the class by using the Journey Method to remember all these words? Hold a contest the next day.

Follow-up ideas

Curriculum-based lesson

When playing 'Break up!' within the curriculum, increase the challenge by allowing the Arrangers to write one key fact each from the subject they are studying on paper for the Models to hold. The Observers must then remember not only the positions but also what the signs said. It may also aid recall later, as the facts will be linked with the visual image of friends in funny positions.

Consider finishing a curriculum lesson every now and then with a quick memory activity. Ask your pupils to call out important words that they have learnt or used in that lesson. List these on the board and get pupils to use the Journey Method to commit the words to memory. When information is more complex than simple lists of words, your pupils will need to:

- Practise identifying key words that trigger longer, more complicated facts.
- Use their imaginations to connect less obvious names or technical vocabulary with visual images, e.g. by thinking of words that sound similar or breaking them up into parts.

The journey method can be used alongside visual mapping tools such as Mind Maps® by hooking each branch or section to a particular room and picturing its key words in different places around that room.

Suggestions for display

 Display your shared 'school journey', using photographs and arrows to show the key points along the route.

Notes for use by other year groups

Practise using this method with younger pupils using simple 3- or 4-step journeys. While it's less likely they would need it for such short lists, gaining familiarity with the method at an early age is useful.

Further resources

 Mind Map® is a registered trademark of The Buzan Organisation Limited 1990. For further information, see *Mind Maps for Kids* by Tony Buzan (2003), London: Thorsons. Also see Year 3, Lesson 3.

List of Year 5 resources provided on the CD Rom

Lesson 1   Metacognition
    Activity sheet: **My Amazing Brain**
    Teacher instructions: **Learning Styles**
    Activity cards: **Learning Styles: I could try … cards**
    Activity sheet: **My brain and how it learns best**

Lesson 2   Questioning
    Teacher instructions: **Catch me if you can** (2 pages, including sample questions)
    Activity cards: **Catch me if you can! Person X and Person Y cards** (2 pages)
    Activity sheet: **What's the question?**
    Activity sheet: **What's the question?** (curriculum follow-up)

Lesson 3   Information skills
    Teacher instructions: **Be a Thinking Detective!** (2 pages)
    Activity sheet: **Be a Thinking Detective!** (2 pages)
    Activity sheet: **Witness Statements**
    Activity sheet: **Crime Hypothesis**

Lesson 4   Critical thinking
    Activity sheet: **Cause and Effect: Multi-Flow Map**
    Activity cards: **Cause and Effect cards**
    Activity sheet: **Cause and Effect: Multi-Flow Map** (for younger pupils)

Lesson 5   Creative thinking
    Activity sheet: **Improve it! Objects**
    Activity sheet: **Improve it! Situations** (curriculum follow-up)

Lesson 6   Decision making
    Activity sheet: **What could it be?**
    Activity sheet: **Reflective Decision Making**
    Activity cards: **Reflective Decision Making cards**

Lesson 7   Memory Skills
Activity sheet: **The Journey Method: Shopping List**

'At a Glance' sample of Year 5 resources

These two pages show a sample selection of activity sheets for this year group. These activities and many more can be found on the CD Rom.

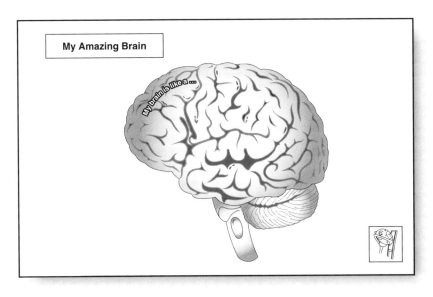

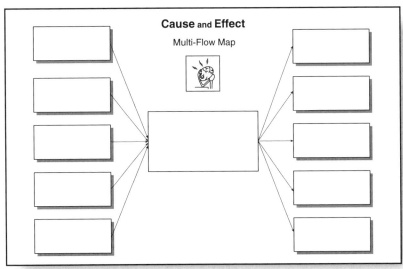

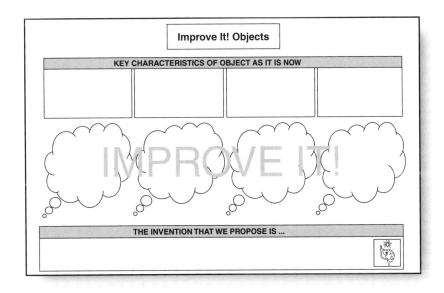

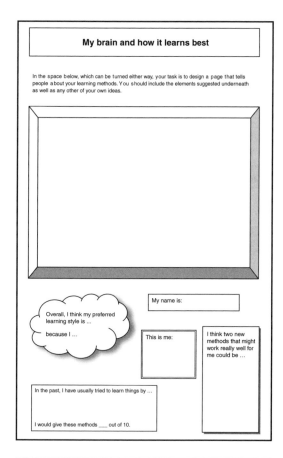

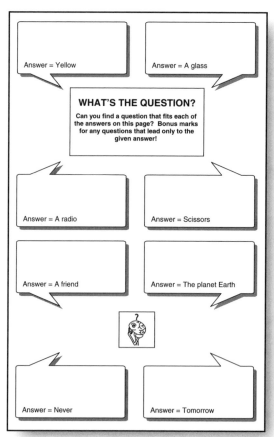

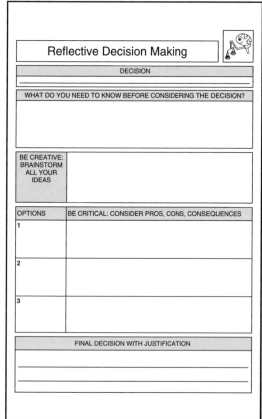

Reflective Decision Making Cards

If you could be any famous person for one day, who would you choose to be?	
You're stranded on a desert island. What one item would you most like to have with you?	
You can invent one new law for the country. What will it be?	
You can take a trip on a magic carpet. Where in this world will you go?	
You can be granted one magic power. What will you choose?	
You can have one new pet and it can be any animal you choose. What will it be?	

Year 6

Lesson plans and resources

Year 6 — Lesson 1

Resources

Activity cards: group sets of **Active Thinking and Learning Dispositions cards** 💿
Teacher instructions: **Our Group's Thinking and Learning Dispositions: sample grid** 💿
Activity sheet: enlarged group copies of **Our Group's Thinking and Learning Dispositions** 💿
Activity sheet: individual copies of **Active Thinking and Learning Dispositions Action Plan** 💿
Activity sheet: individual copies of **Active Thinking and Learning Dispositions Summary Sheet** 💿

Tune in! C Activity: Re-visiting the dispositions

- Share a set of the 'Active Thinking and Learning Disposition' cards among your pupils, so each member has one or two cards.
- Ask your class to sit in a large circle. Explain that they are holding two sets of cards that correspond in some way. Their task is to match up pairs of cards in as short a time as possible, without letting go of or showing anyone the cards they are each holding. Your pupils must decide how best to achieve this.
- Afterwards, ask what the two categories were (names and descriptions of characteristics found to be important in determining a person's success). Briefly discuss the characteristics. Were there any that surprised them? Point out that these characteristics are in many ways more important than what we traditionally think of as 'intelligence' and that they are all qualities we can each – with practice – develop.

Heads together

'Heads together' Introductory session

Page 146

Investigate G5 I Thinking and Learning Tool: Disposition Action Plans

- Give each group a set of the disposition cards and see who can be first to lay them out in pairs.
- Allow a few minutes for the groups to select one volunteer and decide on their 'top 5' dispositions. This should be done quietly so other groups can't hear. The dispositions should be written down in order.
- Write the names of the volunteers on the board. The teams then have 3 minutes to make a 'top 5' list of dispositions for each of the volunteers except their own.
- Taking one volunteer at a time, ask each group to read out their 'top 5'. Award 5 points if their first guess is correct, 4 points if their second is correct and so on. This is a very affirming activity, which should encourage your pupils to think more carefully about their own 'disposition profile'.
- Give each group an enlarged copy of the sheet 'Our Group's Thinking and Learning Dispositions'. Demonstrate how to complete this using the example provided, then allow groups time to discuss and fill in the table.
- Finish by giving each pupil the sheet 'Active Thinking and Learning Dispositions Action Plan'. Ask them to concentrate on 3 dispositions they would most like to develop and record these in the boxes on the right hand side of the sheet. Next, note 3 steps that could be taken to develop each of these qualities.

Emphasise that your pupils are not expected to possess all 20 active thinking and learning qualities now! The 'Keep thinking' task should reveal the lifelong nature of the pursuit of these characteristics. Your pupils are in a strong position as they are learning at an early stage about dispositions that could make a real difference to how they get on in life.

Now reflect!

Questions to consider could include:

- Why do you think we have learned about these dispositions?
- What could you do to maximise your chance of sticking to your action plan?
- How can we support each other (pupils and teacher!) in developing these dispositions?

Keep thinking

Give your pupils a copy of the 'Active Thinking and Learning Dispositions Summary Sheet' to show their parents. Ask them to choose someone at home to interview with 5 questions on the subject of dispositions, e.g.

- Which of the dispositions do you think has helped you the most? Why?
- Which 3 dispositions would you most like to develop?

Follow-up ideas

Unlike the following six lessons, there is no curriculum follow-up for the Metacognition lesson. However, you may still like to try some of the following:

- Ask your pupils to name some famous people whom they admire. Which of the thinking and learning dispositions do they think helped them the most? Make a display with pictures of these people, surrounded by the relevant disposition cards.
- Make a trail of the set of Active Thinking and Learning Disposition Cards. Take photographs of your pupils and give them each three copies of their picture. These can be displayed next to the 3 dispositions that your pupils feel represent their main strengths.
- Use the technique from 'Re-visiting the Dispositions' within the curriculum by creating a set of cards, made up of pairs that match in some way, e.g. half with names of countries and half with capital cities; half with words in a foreign language and half in your own; half with terms and half definitions and so on. Share them among your pupils, not revealing what the two types are, and time them while they work out the categories and match themselves up. Increase the challenge by having one set that contains more ambiguous clues for the other.

Suggestions for display

See 'Follow-up ideas' above.

Further resources

There are many excellent resources to support the development of positive thinking and learning habits. See Chapter 6 in Part One for a list of recommended books and websites.

Year 6   Lesson 2

Resources

Activity sheet: enlarged group copies of **The Question Ladder**

Tune in!   C G4   Activity: Tell me the truth!

- Ask your class to suggest the name of a famous person from the past or present. Invite them to imagine, not only that this person is about to come into the classroom, but that they possess magic powder that will make the person tell only the complete truth. What 3 questions would they ask?
- Allow time for your pupils to discuss this with a partner, then to share their ideas.
- Repeat with another famous person, this time from a History topic that they are studying. Point out that this is where some of the most interesting research begins – with someone asking a question that no one else thought of and then following it up with an investigation

---

Heads together

This lesson: Philosophy for Children, 'Generating the Question Session'   Page 150
Curriculum lesson: Philosophy for Children, 'Discussion Session'   Page 151
Discussion skill: Challenging others to give reasons or examples. Encourage your class to listen closely to each other and to ask people to support their opinions where it will strengthen their argument.

Investigate   G4   Thinking and Learning Tool: The Question Ladder

- Invite each team to select a favourite film or television show. List these on the board and make sure everyone is familiar with them.
- Give each group an enlarged copy of the sheet 'The Question Ladder' and ask them to fill in the subject they have chosen. From the bottom of the sheet, briefly discuss the different levels and types of questioning that exist:

  o Questions that require you simply to remember and repeat facts
  o Questions that ask you to show you have understood something.
  o Questions that invite you to turn information into another form.
  o Questions that ask you to analyse information, make comparisons, sort it into different lists and work out what it means.
  o Questions that require you to use what you have learned to draw inferences or make predictions.
  o Questions that ask you to summarise what you think by reaching an opinion or making a decision.

- Allow 10 minutes for the groups to work together to devise a quiz sheet about their chosen show that includes one question from each level. They should keep a record of any factual answers that are required and note ideas for answers to more open-ended questions.
- Swap the sheets around and allow a further 15 minutes for teams to work on their answers.

- The sheets should then be returned to their original groups for 'assessment'. Ask groups to provide a feedback sheet for each other, showing which answers are correct and noting comments about more open tasks.

While favourite films and television shows prove popular as a topic, many other subjects would work equally well with this exercise. 'The Question Ladder' can also be used by teachers, to help ensure that verbal and written questioning is sufficiently varied and challenging.

Now reflect!

Questions to consider could include:
- Why do you think we did this activity?
- Why is it important to ask questions?
- Which type of question is most common in school? Which type made you think the hardest? Which type do you find the most interesting?

Keep thinking

If you had magic question powder that would make a person tell the complete truth, who would you choose to use it on? What would you ask? Why? This activity makes a very interesting display.

Follow-up ideas

Curriculum-based lesson

'Tell me the truth!' is a great activity to personalise History topics in particular, but can also be used with religious figures, artists, authors or characters from books. For a further creative alternative, try applying it to inanimate objects, getting your pupils, for example, to think of questions they would ask a pineapple, a bridge or a camera. This then has further curriculum possibilities, as interesting questions might be asked of subject-based items, such as a light bulb, a plant or a magnet.

One good way of devising a curriculum lesson that makes use of 'The Question Ladder' is to provide each group with a different passage covering an important aspect of your subject, whether in Science, Geography, History, Religious Studies etc. By getting your pupils to set the questions themselves, you oblige them to develop a thorough understanding of the passage, so this can act as a useful way of covering a range of different areas in a short amount of time or as a revision exercise towards the end of a topic. Swap sheets as before, then conclude the lesson with each group presenting their answers to the rest of the class.

If your pupils are studying a particular book, this can be an interesting way to get them to focus on the chapter or section they have just read. Similarly it can focus attention on a newspaper article. Once your pupils are more familiar with the different question 'steps', it's also an excellent method of encouraging them to pay close attention while watching a recording of a television programme or listening to a radio broadcast.

Suggestions for display

An interesting display can be made, with the subject at the bottom (e.g. a photocopy of the cover of the book that the class is studying) and the different rungs of the ladder above, each with questions provided by the pupils. This is particularly effective with a real ladder.

Further resources

This activity is loosely based on Bloom's taxonomy.

Resources

Teacher instructions: **What's it all about?** ✏
Teacher instructions: **Yes/No Tree Diagrams – sample diagram** ✏
Activity sheet: Enlarged group copies of **Yes/No Tree Diagrams** ✏
You will need to find: 5 sheets of A4 plain paper

Tune in!	D G3	Activity: What's it all about?

- Read the practice example provided on the sheet, 'What's it all about?' to the class twice at normal speed, encouraging them to listen carefully and allowing them to note key points the second time.
- Ask your pupils to suggest what the main points were and record their phrases on the board. Together, find a way of combining these in less than 20 words. Compare the class answer with the suggestion provided.
- Repeat with the two passages provided, this time giving groups 3 minutes to work together to come up with each summary. Share answers.
- Ask your class what the purpose of this activity was. Was it necessary to understand every word?

Heads together	

This lesson: Philosophy for Children, 'Generating the Question Session'   Page 150
Curriculum lesson: Philosophy for Children, 'Discussion Session'   Page 151
Discussion skill: Challenging others to give reasons or examples. Encourage your class to listen closely to each other and to ask people to support their opinions where it will strengthen their argument.

Investigate	D G4	Thinking and Learning Tool: Yes/No Tree Diagrams

- Ask your class to suggest 5 types of food and choose volunteers to draw and label these on separate pieces of paper. Stick the pictures along the bottom of the board.
- Ask your pupils to think of a question for which the answer would be Yes for some of the types of food displayed and No for others. Write this near the top of the board and draw two branches – one for yes and one for no – below it. See example on sheet 'Yes/No Tree Diagrams: Sample Diagram'.
- As a class, decide which pictures can be sorted and stuck below each of the branches, then focus on one of the groups and repeat the activity, finding a second question to sort them further. Continue until you have a complete diagram that sorts all 5 types of food.
- Give each group the sheet 'Yes/No Tree Diagrams' and ask them to choose a category of people, e.g. pop stars, actors, football players, cartoon characters etc.
- Get them to brainstorm 8 to 10 names of people within their category and note these in the space provided. Their task is to devise a 'Yes/No Tree Diagram' to identify the people they have chosen, by working out a series of questions of the type used in the example. Final answers should not be filled in.

- Swap sheets and allow time for the groups to use the Tree Diagram they have received to sort the characters noted at the top of the sheet. This should then be presented to the class. The original group can declare whether the answers are correct or not.

> Devising Yes/No Tree Diagrams is a useful way of encouraging your pupils to think carefully about the key characteristics of different objects, people or places, which builds on activities done in earlier years.

Now reflect!

Questions to consider could include:

- When might it be useful to get the 'gist' of a piece of text?
- What sort of thinking skills did you use when making the Tree Diagrams?
- Can you think of anything else that could be sorted using this type of diagram?

Keep thinking

Make a Yes/No Tree Diagram to sort the characters in your favourite television programme, the people in a favourite band or the members of your family.

Follow-up ideas

Curriculum-based lesson

When playing 'What's it all about?' again, three options are possible:

1 Develop pupils' language skills by getting them to write their own short silly passages that can be used for the activity.
2 Use it to help your pupils gain practice with summarising skills within the curriculum, by giving them a series of short texts from book, magazine articles or an encyclopaedia.
3 Try it as a revision strategy. Give each group responsibility for an aspect of the topic and challenge them to summarise its key points within a given word limit. These can then be passed around so that following groups have a chance to improve them further. Final summaries can be read out, checked and recorded on a revision sheet for the whole class.

Yes/No Tree Diagrams can usefully be devised within several different subjects. Either give your pupils a set of picture or name cards or ask them to brainstorm these themselves at the beginning of the lesson. Then get them to work together in groups to carry out the necessary research to sort the different items. A few examples could include:

- Science – different plants, animals, materials, planets
- Maths – three-dimensional shapes, numbers
- History – the wives of Henry VIII, Greek gods and goddesses, famous people in Victorian times
- English – characters in a book
- Art – paintings or sculptures by a given artist

Suggestions for display

 As an extension activity, challenge your more able pupils to make a large display version of the Yes/No Tree Diagram to sort all the members of the class or their idols.

Year 6

Lesson 4

Resources

Activity Sheet: enlarged group copies of **Layers of Inference** (2 pages)
Activity sheet: **Layers of Inference** (curriculum follow-up)

Tune in!   C   Activity: Amazing but true!

- Ask your class to stand in a circle.
- Present them with one amazing fact at a time and work around the circle, asking each pupil in turn to give a sentence beginning either:
  - o It must be true that ... (definite conclusion)
  - o It may be true that ... (possible conclusion).
- Challenge a selection of both correct and incorrect responses, involving everyone in deciding whether they represent definite or merely possible conclusions. Some (apparently true) facts to use are:
  - o Pigs can be trained to do the same tricks as dogs
  - o The silkworm moth has 11 brains
  - o On average, women utter 7000 words per day compared to a man's 2000.

Heads together

This lesson:	Philosophy for Children, 'Generating the Question Session'	Page 150
Curriculum lesson:	Philosophy for Children, 'Discussion Session'	Page 151
Discussion skill:	Recognising opinions from facts. Encourage your pupils to make the distinction clear, for example by using the words, 'In my opinion ...' and 'It is true that ...'.	

Investigate   G4   Thinking and Learning Tool: Layers of Inference

- Point out that the main activity follows on from 'Amazing but true', as it requires your pupils to draw both definite conclusions and possible inferences.
- Give each group an enlarged copy of the first 'Layers of Inference' sheet and invite them to look closely at the picture in the middle.
- Clarify the fact that the words 'conclusion' and 'inference' both mean something that you work out as being either definitely or possibly true, based on available evidence.
- Explain that their task is to consider first of all whether the source picture tells them anything that is definitely true. Share a few ideas, then allow time for the groups to note their thoughts inside the first layer of the diagram.
- Repeat with the second layer: What *possible* conclusions can be drawn from the photograph?
- Finally, ask your class to spend some time discussing what else they might like to find out about the scene in the photograph and to note their questions in the outer box.
- While your pupils are working on this, circulate to make sure they understand the different categories.
- At the end, share ideas.

- Repeat the activity with the second 'Layers of Inference' sheet, this time allowing groups to work more independently.

> Even older children tend to find both activities surprisingly challenging and will need support in learning to recognise the difference between definite and possible conclusions. In both cases, rather than simply correcting them, respond positively to all ideas but try to probe your pupils' thinking. Ask them to explain their reasoning and see if they can come up with situations where their apparently definite conclusion might not, in fact, hold.

Now reflect!

Questions to consider could include:

- Was it useful to repeat the 'Layers of Inference' activity twice? If so, why? What was different second time round?
- What skills were required?
- When might these skills be useful in other situations and subjects?

Keep thinking

What definite conclusions could a visitor draw from visiting this classroom? What possible conclusions might they draw?

Follow-up ideas

Curriculum-based lesson

Follow the same format for 'Amazing but true', but prepare a list of interesting facts that fit within a curriculum topic. This works particularly well for Science and History, but can also be used in other contexts. Carry this out verbally or as a written exercise, with pairs or small groups of pupils working together to think about the statements. Alternatively, each group could take responsibility for just one of the statements and present their ideas to class.

'Layers of Inference' provides an excellent way of encouraging your pupils to develop their observation and logical thinking skills. Use the blank 'Layers of Inference' sheet provided and link with virtually any subject, focusing on one of the following:

- A photograph
- A picture
- A set of statistics
- A graph or table
- An advertisement
- A piece of text, such as an article, diary extract, letter or passage from a book

Decide whether you would like the whole class to focus on the same 'source' or whether different groups should look at different areas, then present their ideas to the rest of the group.

Suggestions for display

Devote an area of the classroom to 'Layers of Inference', with a new source displayed each week for your students to look at. Supply slips of paper or self-adhesive notes for your pupils to write their ideas on and stick them to the appropriate layer of the display.

Further resources

The 'Layers of Inference' tool was described by C. Riley in the article 'Evidential Understanding, period knowledge and the development of literacy: a practical approach to "layers of inference" for Key Stage 3' in *Teaching History*, Issue 97, November 1999. It was initially developed by Hilary Cooper in her book *The Teaching of History in Primary Schools* (1992), London: David Fulton Publishers.

Resources

Activity sheet: enlarged group copies of **Random Input Problem Solving** 💿
You will need to find: Small slips of paper and several old magazines

Tune in!   C   Activity: Absurd Analogies

- Give each pupil a slip of paper and ask them to write a simple activity, such as 'playing football', 'buying shoes' or 'climbing a tree'. These should be collected in and placed in a box or hat.
- Invite two volunteers to pick out a slip each and to read them to the class.
- Your pupils' task is to think of as many ways as possible in which these two events are similar. For instance, if the question was 'In what ways is "catching flu" like "jumping on a trampoline"', possible answers could include 'both make you feel tired', 'both often happen outdoors' and 'both can cause dizziness'.
- Repeat with further pairs of activities picked from the box. You may wish to turn this into a team competition by awarding a point for every answer.

Heads together

This lesson:	Philosophy for Children, 'Generating the Question Session'	Page 150
Curriculum lesson:	Philosophy for Children, 'Discussion Session'	Page 151
Discussion skill:	Recognising opinions from facts. Encourage your pupils to make the distinction clear, for example by using the words, 'In my opinion ...' and 'It is true that ...'	

Investigate   G4   Thinking and Learning Tool: Random Input Problem Solving

- Ask your class to imagine the situation: you need to plan a charity fund-raising event that will be a great success, but which no one else has ever done before. People are getting bored of the normal events, so it's up to you to be creative and come up with something entirely new. The problem is – you've gone blank! Explain that the method they are going to learn today is particularly useful for situations when your imagination lets you down and when you need a really unusual idea.
- Give each group one or two old magazines and an enlarged copy of the sheet 'Random Input Problem Solving'.
- Ask your pupils to turn to a page and randomly pick one word or picture. They should note this in the first central box on their sheet.
- What ideas could this lead to? Encourage your class to think laterally and to use this word or picture to stimulate new ideas. Allow time for them to brainstorm and record four possible fund-raising options. Then ask them to select the best and to record this in the box below.

- Repeat this twice more with different random inputs.
- At the end, each group should decide which is their best overall idea and present this in a 'sales pitch' to the rest of the class.

Emphasise the fact that new ideas rarely come 'out of the blue'. Often they are simply an adapted or improved version of something that already exists and even when they genuinely appear to arrive from nowhere, our brains have often been triggered by something we have seen, heard or read. The Random Input method simply formalizes this.

Now reflect!

Questions to consider could include:

- What do you think of this method of creative thinking?
- Can you think of any other occasions when it might be useful?
- Could it ever help in school? How?

Keep thinking

Give each pupil 5 pieces of card the size of playing cards and ask them to help make a class set of 'Random Input Ideas cards'. These could include unusual headlines from newspapers, interesting pictures from magazines, quotes, favourite words – anything that might spur a creative idea. The set could then be used for future creative activities or when a pupil is stuck for an idea when writing a story or poem.

Follow-up ideas

Curriculum-based lesson

The Random Input method probably applies best to English, but could also be used to help develop creative ideas within art or design and technology.

One activity is to use it when writing stories. Have a selection of magazines and newspapers on each group's table and invite each pupil to randomly pick a word or picture. This should be written in the middle of a plain piece of paper. Get your pupils to make a second selection and write or stick it onto the page somewhere near the first. Encourage them to think about how the two words might be connected and whether, together, they might provide a stimulus for a story idea. Your pupils should use their sheet to note any ideas, connections and story-lines that they come up with, then repeat this activity as many times as they wish. Each time, new ideas can be added and old, less successful ones can be altered or weeded out. After this initial ideas period, encourage your pupils to write a brief outline of their story's main events. This can then be used as a reminder when writing the real story.

If possible, find real-life problem solving contexts to which your pupils can apply the technique. For example, could they plan and carry out a real fund-raising event, a class party or an activity for a younger year group?

Suggestions for display

Have a Random Input Creativity Corner where you mount a changing set of display cards and pictures alongside challenges such as 'Invent something today!', 'Write a poem!', 'Begin a new club' and 'Make up a game!'

Resources

Teacher instructions: **Opening Up the Options** 💿
Activity cards: one set of **Opening Up the Options scenario cards** 💿
Activity sheet: enlarged group copies of **Opening Up the Options** 💿
You will need to find: sheets of plain paper

Tune in!	C	Activity: Up in the Air

- Ask your pupils to write, in the centre of a piece of paper, a completely made up dilemma, e.g.
  - Should I be a pop singer of a famous tennis player?
  - Should I dye my hair purple or green?
  - Should I buy a yacht or a racehorse?
- Ask them to turn the sheet into a paper aeroplane, then on the count of three to throw it 'up in the air' in any direction across the class.
- Everyone should pick up a plane, open it and add a 'useful' (though probably silly!) comment regarding the decision, for example 'purple is often thought of as a royal colour, so is better than green'. This could be additional information, relevant advice or a possible solution.
- Repeat several times, then return the sheets to their original owners to look at. Can they make a decision that takes account of the information gathered?

Heads together		

This lesson:	Philosophy for Children, 'Generating the Question Session'	Page 150
Curriculum lesson:	Philosophy for Children, 'Discussion Session'	Page 151
Discussion skill:	Using persuasive language. Encourage your pupils to make use of persuasive phrases and to recognise them in other people's comments.	

Investigate	D G4	Thinking and Learning Tool: Opening Up the Options

- Explain that we're often presented with 'either–or' situations where it seems as though we have to make a difficult choice between two options. Ask your class for examples of situations that they have faced where they felt they had to choose between two options. How did they make their decision?
- Summarise the methods described. Point out that good decision makers will often take the logical approach and consider both options by weighing up their good and bad points (their 'pros' and 'cons') and by considering the consequences. However, people frequently forget that creative thinking also aids decision making. Instead of accepting that the decision *must* be between the two options, we could consider two further possibilities:
  - Finding a compromise solution that involves elements of both options.
  - Thinking of an entirely new solution that means you don't have to make the initial choice.
- Give each group one of the 'Opening Up the Options scenario cards'. Allow them time to read their cards and to ensure that all members understand the situation and the 'either–or' decision with which they're faced.

- Give out copies of the sheet 'Opening Up the Options' and follow the teacher instructions provided for the activity.
- Afterwards, groups should take turns to present their ideas by reading out their scenario card, describing or acting out the four options they considered and explaining which one they felt was the best overall.

If possible, tell your class about an experience of your own where you found yourself having to choose between two options. Could the 'Opening Up the Options' method have helped? Enlist their help in coming up with alternative solutions.

Now reflect!

Questions to consider could include:

- What does it mean when we say something is 'up in the air'?
- Can you think of any decisions you have to make that are still 'up in the air'?
- Now that you have done the main activity, can you come up with any creative alternatives to the two options you faced in the 'either–or' decisions you mentioned earlier?

Keep thinking

Ask your pupils to interview someone at home about a situation where they had to make a difficult decision between two options and where they needed to think creatively about compromise solutions or alternative possibilities.

Follow-up ideas

Curriculum-based lesson

The 'Up in the Air' method is a good way of sharing ideas and gathering facts and opinions about a wide range of topics. It can be used either to find out what pupils know at the beginning of a topic or as a revision exercise at the end. Play it with groups and allocate each team a topic within your chosen subject. Give them one minute to write the topic title in the middle of the sheet and to brainstorm ideas around it. Throw the sheet – either as a ball or a plane – to another team, who should be given two minutes to read the comments already on the sheet and add any further ideas. Repeat, increasing the time for each round, until all teams have contributed to all sheets, then return them to the original group to present the key points to the class.

The 'Opening Up the Options' tool suits environmental and social topics very well. For example, older pupils might be interested to consider issues such as:

- whether we should have nuclear fuel or rely on further supplies of natural gas and oil
- whether we should allow or ban fox hunting
- whether we should encourage or restrict immigration
- whether we should test products on animals or make this practice illegal

In each of these cases, it's worth considering the pros and cons of the two opposite solutions, before moving on to think about compromise solutions and completely new creative ideas. Groups could be allocated a 'dilemma' each and given time to carry out the research and analysis stages, then be invited to present their findings and suggestions to the class.

Suggestions for display

Display a sign reminding your pupils to 'Watch out for "either–or" situations!' Encourage them to bring in articles from newspapers where an overly simplistic analysis may lead people to assume that just two options are possible.

Resources

Activity sheet: individual copies of **Number Hooks**
You will need to find: plain paper and masking tape

| **T**une in! | C | Activity: It's a mad world! |

- Ask your pupils to imagine a world completely different to ours and to write one secret 'fact' about it on a piece of paper, e.g. the sky is green; children teach adults; cats run all the supermarkets. This should be attached to their back with masking tape.
- Allow two minutes for pupils to wander around the class, reading and remembering as many facts as they can.
- When the time's up, everyone returns to their seats and records what they recall.
- Get your pupils to take turns to read out the fact that they invented, while everyone awards themselves one point for each fact correctly remembered. Add up scores.
- Remind pupils that our short-term memories hold very few pieces of information before 'overflowing' and discarding old facts as new ones enter. Special methods are needed to make memories 'stick'. Discuss any tactics devised by pupils.

| **H**eads together | | |

This lesson:	Philosophy for Children, 'Generating the Question Session'	Page 150
Curriculum lesson:	Philosophy for Children, 'Discussion Session'	Page 151
Discussion skill:	Using persuasive language. Encourage your pupils to make use of persuasive phrases and to recognise them in other people's comments.	

| **I**nvestigate | D G2 C | Thinking and Learning Tool: Number Hooks |

- Explain that the Number Hooks technique works by helping you 'hook' new information to pictures already stored in your long-term memory. One commonly used series of pictures are those linked with the numbers 1 to 10. Give the sheet 'Number Hooks' to each pupil.
- Read through the list of rhymes and allow a few minutes for your pupils to fix these in their minds, finding alternative rhymes for numbers if they prefer.
- Ask them to call out random words and make a list of 10 of these on the board. Demonstrate the method with the first word. For example, if it was 'cucumber', you might imagine the **sun** (number **one**) with cucumber rays of light beaming out of it in all directions. Images should be as colourful, exaggerated and absurd as possible.
- Allow time for your pupils to work in pairs to develop 10 visual images that link the number rhymes with the words on the board. These should be noted on the sheet.
- Rub out the words on the board and test your class by asking them to cover their sheets and call out what the third word was, what the tenth and so on.

- Point out that often we have to remember longer facts rather than simple words. In this case, they need to pick out a key word that helps trigger the fact or develop an image that links two or three ideas. Use sentences from the 'It's a mad world!' game as examples, e.g.
    o (Sun) The sky is green. Picture the sun beaming green light across the sky.
    o (Shoe) Children teach adults. Picture a class full of adults at desks with shoes on their heads.
    o (Tree) Cats run all the supermarkets. Picture a supermarket with a tree in each aisle for cats to scratch their claws on.
- Finish by repeating the 'It's a mad world!' game, this time using the Number Hooks method.

> This activity relies on your pupils being able to form strong visual images of the type practised in the Visual Images, Story Method and Journey Method sessions in Years 3, 4 and 5. If they have not done these sessions, you may want to introduce these methods beforehand.

Now reflect!

Questions to consider could include:

- What are the strengths of the Number Hooks method? (e.g. ability to remember items in order; could combine numbers to go beyond 10; simple but effective)
- What might its weaknesses be? (e.g. would it be harder to apply to complex information?)
- When could it be useful at school?

Keep thinking

Ask your pupils to invent more quick memory games that could be played at home or school. Make a class book of games that could be reproduced and given to each pupil.

Follow-up ideas

Curriculum-based lesson

As it is rare that pupils have to learn simple lists of words, you will need to support them in learning to apply this memory technique to more complex information. Try these two revision strategies, beginning with the first, easier, one then encouraging greater independence with the second.

(1) Devise a set of facts that summarise your topic and supply your pupils with one each. Use the 'It's a mad world!' technique, combined with the Journey Method (Year 5) or Number Hooks, to gather and recall as many facts as possible in a given amount of time.

(2) Get your pupils to work in pairs or groups to work out how a subject can be 'telescoped' into 10 important pieces of information. They should draw a table with three columns, listing their pieces of information in the first column. In the second column, they pick out one key word from each piece of information that will act as a trigger to help them remember the fact. In the third, they use the Number Hooks method to note visual images to help them recall the key words.

Suggestions for display

Display the numbers 1 to 10, together with a bold, clear picture of each rhyming word. Refer to this and use the method whenever appropriate in other lessons. For example, at the end of a lesson, ask your pupils what the three main points were that they learnt. Draw out key words and link them with the number pictures on display.

List of Year 6 resources provided on the CD Rom

Lesson 1   Metacognition
    Activity cards: **Active Thinking and Learning Dispositions cards** (3 pages)
    Teacher instructions: **Our Group's Thinking and Learning Dispositions: sample grid**
    Activity sheet: **Our Group's Thinking and Learning Dispositions**
    Activity sheet: **Active Thinking and Learning Dispositions Action Plan**
    Activity sheet: **Active Thinking and Learning Dispositions Summary Sheet**

Lesson 2   Questioning
    Activity sheet: **The Question Ladder**

Lesson 3   Information skills
    Teacher instructions: **What's it all about?**
    Teacher instructions: **Yes/No Tree Diagrams: sample diagram**
    Activity sheet: **Yes/No Tree Diagrams**

Lesson 4   Critical thinking
    Activity sheet: **Layers of Inference** (2 pages)
    Activity sheet: **Layers of Inference** (curriculum follow-up)

Lesson 5   Creative thinking
    Activity sheet: **Random Input Problem Solving**

Lesson 6   Decision making
    Teacher instructions: **Opening Up the Options**
    Activity sheet: **Opening Up the Options**
    Activity cards: **Opening Up the Options scenario cards**

Lesson 7   Memory Skills
    Activity sheet: **Number Hooks**

'At a Glance' sample of Year 6 resources

These two pages show a sample selection of activity sheets for this year group.
These activities and many more can be found on the CD Rom.

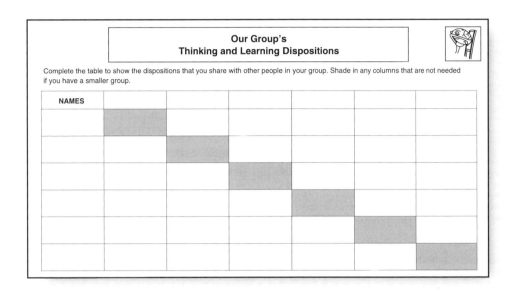

Our Group's Thinking and Learning Dispositions

Complete the table to show the dispositions that you share with other people in your group. Shade in any columns that are not needed if you have a smaller group.

NAMES						

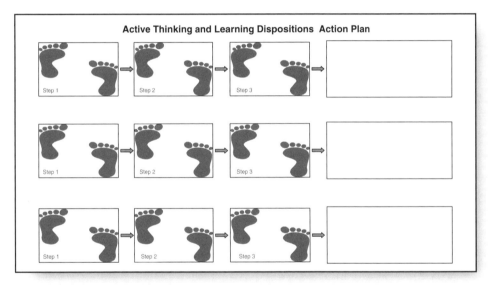

Active Thinking and Learning Dispositions Action Plan

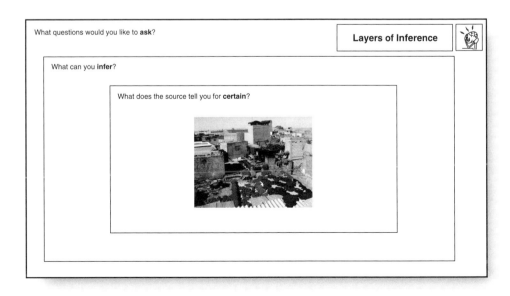

What questions would you like to **ask**?

Layers of Inference

What can you **infer**?

What does the source tell you for **certain**?

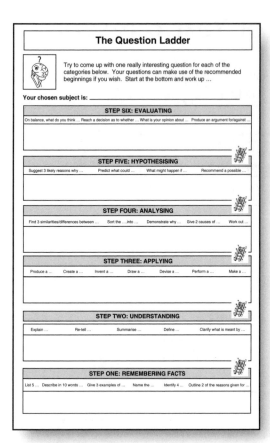

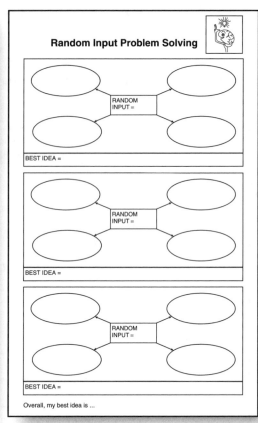

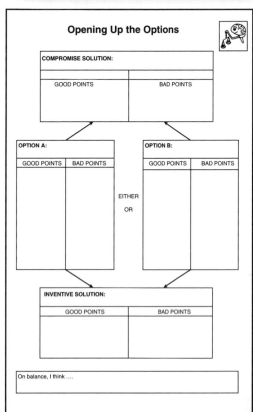

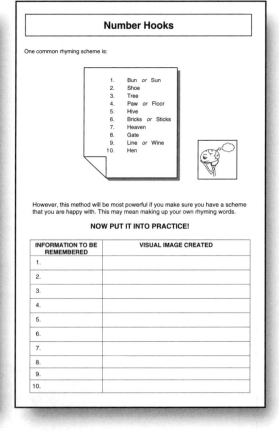

Part Three

General Resources for All Year Groups

'At a Glance' sample of general resources

This page shows a sample selection of general resources for use with all year groups. These and many more can be found full size on the CD Rom.

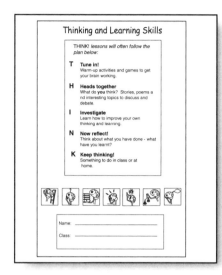

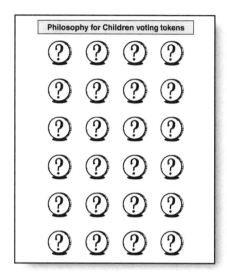

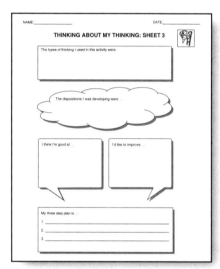

'Heads together' resources

'Heads together' Introductory Session

1. Explain that good thinkers enjoy having good discussions. But what is a good discussion? Ask your pupils for ideas. One way to clarify this is to ask them what makes a bad discussion (an example of the 'Reverse Decision Making' method used in Year 3, Lesson 5), as this tends to be easier to answer. Ideas might include:

A good discussion is one where:

- people listen to each other
- everyone gets a turn
- it's about an interesting topic

A bad discussion is one where:

- people feel afraid to speak
- people talk while others are talking
- you get laughed at if people disagree with you

2. Tell your class that this first lesson will be used to decide on some rules to make sure that they always have a good discussion rather than a bad one.

3. Ask the pupils for suggestions for rules. With Year 1, it works well to ask the class's 'thinking toy'. What he/she thinks should be the first rule and ask the children what they think of this suggestion. With older pupils, you might use the 'Think – Pair – Share' routine'. ✎ This involves giving your pupils a few moments to think quietly and to note down any ideas that they have, before linking with a partner and deciding together on one or two 'best' rules. These are then shared with the whole class and the full list is written on the board, using positive 'we will' statements rather than negative ones where possible.

4. Vote together for the rules the class feel are most important. Sample rules are included on page 147, but it is strongly suggested that your pupils generate their own list themselves and that they limit themselves to about six to eight rules.

5. Encourage your class to choose their own 'thinking signal' to show that they would like to contribute something to the discussion.

✎ The 'Think – Pair – Share' routine was developed by Harvard's Project Zero group and is described in the 'Visible Thinking' section of their website:

http://www.pz.harvard.edu/vt/VisibleThinking_html_files/01_VisibleThinkingInAction/01a_VTInAction.html. It was adapted from the work of Frank Lyman (Lyman, 1981).

Sample class rules for 'Heads together' discussions

Key Stage 1

We will:

- Let everyone have a turn
- Listen to each other
- Think carefully
- Be brave with our ideas
- Value what others have to say
- Give reasons for what we believe

Key Stage 2

We have agreed that:

- We will encourage everyone to join in
- We will be confident and contribute our own ideas
- We will listen and learn from each other's points of view
- We will show respect for what people say and not laugh, interrupt or put them down just because we disagree
- We will wait until a person has finished talking before we signal that we have something to say
- We will explain how what we say fits with what has already been said and will always try to give our reasons. For example:

  'I agree/disagree with ... because ...'

  'I would like to add something else to what ... said, because I think that ...'
- We will stop and think about what people are saying, so we try to understand what they mean, even when they are not very clear
- We will ask people to explain what they mean if we are not sure we have understood something
- We will be prepared to change our mind if we hear someone else put forward a valid opinion, rather than sticking with a fixed point of view
- When we reach a decision, we will make sure we have legitimate reasons to support our opinions
- We will stay calm and enjoy the discussion!

'Heads together' suggested topics and stimuli

Robert Fisher writes:

> A stimulus is the presentation of a starting point for enquiry. The chosen stimulus should provide a kind of dramatic setting for the enquiry. It should provide what the philosopher Whitehead called Romance, that is something to stimulate the creative, critical or imaginative response of the student. The stimulus provides the challenging context for thinking. It aims to offer a positive cognitive intervention that will engage attention and stimulate enquiry. The starting point should be complex or challenging enough to repay close and focused attention. (2003: 172)

Whatever the subject you choose, it is important to keep up a good pace during discussions, to give everyone a chance to speak and to summarise their ideas at the end. 'Heads together' sessions need not be very long: indeed, it is probably better to keep them shorter so all pupils stay focused, interested and involved.

Moral dilemmas

These make ideal topics for debate for two reasons.

First, they are relevant for children who may be facing worrying situations and who are finding their way in a life full of decisions and potential dangers. Children need to be provided with the intellectual means to make informed decisions about the values that they will build throughout their lives.

Secondly, by debating issues for which there is no black or white, no right or wrong, no absolutes, we create for pupils a less threatening environment in which to begin to explore and develop their own ideas.

Examples could relate to day-to-day life or topics in the news. For instance:

Day-to-day life

- What would you do if a friend told you she had stolen something?
- Your friends laugh at you because you won't try a cigarette. What should you do?
- Is telling the truth always the right thing to do?

In the news

- Should animal testing be made illegal?
- Who is responsible for the environment?
- Is it right to allow whale hunting?

It is a good idea to make a collection of short stories and articles that could be used to prompt these sorts of debate. A very useful educational resource that takes topical news stories and presents them with detailed suggestions for use in the classroom can be found at: http://www.dialogueworks.co.uk/newswise/.

Although this is a subscription service, several sample editions are available to view.

Poems and stories

Short stories and poems raise all sorts of interesting questions – about characters, motivations, ambiguities and underlying themes. Robert Fisher has compiled several excellent collections, two of which are:

- Fisher, R. (1996) *Stories for Thinking*. Oxford: Nash Pollock
- Fisher, R. (1997) *Poems for Thinking*. Oxford: Nash Pollock

Objects and artefacts

Objects and artefacts provoke fascinating curriculum-based discussions, as can pictures, sculptures and photographs. Questions could include:

- What do you think might be taking place outside this picture?
- What may have happened just before this photograph was taken?
- How many possible uses might this object have?

Music and film

Listening to any kind of music – classical, jazz, global, popular – is another excellent way of spurring a discussion, as is showing a short excerpt from a film, a documentary, a newsreel or an advertisement.

Real or hypothetical situations

For a slightly different sort of discussion, present your class with a hypothetical situation to debate, such as:

- Children should be allowed to go to school as and when they wish.
- People should pass a test before becoming parents.
- Everyone should have a day off on their birthday.

Alternatively, begin by setting the scene, which may be real or imagined, then present your class with a problem to solve. For example:

- Litter is a real problem in our school. What could we do about it?
- We need to raise money for our local hospital. What should we do?
- Some argue that, during the long summer holiday, children tend to forget a lot of what they have learned. What could be done about this?

Philosophy for Children: Generating the Question Session

1. Ask the pupils to re-cap the rules that were agreed by the class and discuss these briefly again if needed.

2. Introduce a stimulus passage, short story, poem, article, object or picture and explain that it will be up to the class to choose a really interesting question that is linked to this topic. See 'Heads together: suggested resources' for ideas regarding selection of this stimulus. Point out that this means your pupils will need to listen or look very thoughtfully.

3. Read or show the discussion prompt to the class.

4. Use the 'Think – Pair – Share' routine to generate questions linked with the focus topic. Encourage your pupils to think about what was particularly interesting or puzzling about the stimulus. Each pupil or pair of pupils should have the chance to contribute their best question. Write these on the board.

5. There are many possible ways of choosing a question and ideally your pupils should discuss the different methods that are available. One simple method is to conduct a vote to choose the focus for discussion. You could use voting tokens. ✪ As each question is called out, those pupils wishing to vote for it could bring you their token.

6. Keep the question displayed prominently until the next lesson.

Philosophy for Children: Discussion Session

1. Discussions work best when everyone is comfortable and can see each other. Sitting in a circle on chairs or on the floor in the school library, hall or in your classroom if you have sufficient space is often better than remaining seated at individual or group desks.

2. Begin by asking the pupils to remind you of the focus that was considered. For instance, they may be able to remember the main stages of a story, the topic of a poem or the key features of a picture.

3. Read out the question that was chosen and remind your pupils of their 'Heads together' class rules.

4. The table on page 34 in Part Two, 'Heads Together: Development of Skills', shows a progression of discussion skills, which can be introduced gradually across the year groups should this suit your school. These are also noted on the individual lesson plans. If you choose to follow this progression, explain the communication skill that will be important for this lesson.

5. Oversee the discussion, encouraging as many pupils to contribute as possible, valuing all contributions and ensuring that the class rules are upheld. Intervene only where necessary – to maintain the focus, to challenge, to encourage rigour of thought, to improve definitions, to praise pupils for their ideas and contributions and to help the discussion move forward. Sample intervention prompts could include:

   • Expanding: Can you explain that a bit further? Tell me more about …
   • Probing: What is your reason for thinking that? Is that always the case?
   • Encouraging responses: What do you think of what X has just said? Does anyone disagree with that?
   • Focusing: How does that relate to our question? Does this help us answer our question?

6. To foster an environment in which all your pupils learn the value of listening as well as responding, two excellent strategies are proposed by Robert Fisher (2003). One is to give each of your pupils 5 tokens, one of which they must place down whenever they speak. Another is to divide the class into two halves, with one half acting as observers and noting the strengths and weaknesses of the discussion.

7. At the end of the discussion, it is a good idea to go around the circle or group and give everyone an opportunity to sum up what they think about the issue or simply to give some 'last words'. If any were acting as observers, they should be given a chance to feed back to the rest of the group.

References

Part One

Chapter 1

De Bono, E. (1992) *Teach Your Child How to Think*. London: Penguin
McPeck, J. (1990) *Teaching Critical Thinking*. New York/London: Routledge

Chapter 2

Chartier, Emile [Alain] (1938) *Propos sur la religion*. Paris: Rieder (reissued 1951, Paris: PUF)
Claxton, G. (1997) *Hare Brain, Tortoise Mind*. London: Fourth Estate
Costa, A. (2002) Presentation to 10th International Conference on Thinking. Harrogate, United Kingdom
De Botton, A. (2000) *The Consolations of Philosophy*. London: Penguin
Fisher, R. (2003) *Teaching Thinking: Philosophical Enquiry in the Classroom*, 2nd edn. London: Continuum (1st edn, 1998)
Fisher, R. (2002) Presentation 10th International Conference on Thinking. Harrogate, United Kingdom
Quinn, V. (1997) *Critical Thinking in Young Minds*. London: David Fulton
Von Oech, R. (1998) *A Whack on the Side of the Head*. New York: Warner Books

Chapter 3

Claxton, G. (2002) *Building Learning Power: Helping Young People to Become Good Learners*. Bristol: TLO
Skinner, B.F. (1964) 'Education in 1984', *New Scientist*, 21 May

Chapter 5

Cam, P. (1995) *Thinking Together: Philosophical Enquiry in the Classroom*, 2nd edn. London: Continuum
Fisher, R. (2003) *Teaching Thinking: Philosophers*. London: RoutledgeFalmer
Hayes, J. (2002) *Children as Philosophers*. London: RoutledgeFalmer
Splitter, L. and Sharp, A. (1995) *Teaching for Better Thinking: The Classroom Community of Enquiry*. Melbourne: Australian Council for Education Research

Chapter 6

Claxton, G. (2002) *Building Learning Power: Helping Young People to Become Good Learners*. Bristol: TLO
Covey, S. (1989) *The Seven Habits of Highly Effective People*. New York: Simon & Schuster

Part Two

References to books and websites that support the theories and tools used are included in the individual lesson plans.

Part Three

Lyman, F.T. (1981) The responsive classroom discussion: the inclusion of all students. In A. Anderson (ed.) *Mainstreaming Digest*. College Park: University of Maryland Press. pp. 109–113

Fisher, R. (2003) *Teaching Thinking: Philosophical Enquiry in the Classroom*, 2nd edn. London: Continuum

Index